D1144348

THE
REAL GOLDEN AGE
OF MURDER

Pistols, Bombs and Motor Bandits

Published by Robin Books
London

Copyright © 2022 Joan Lock
All rights reserved

Joan Lock has asserted her right
under the Copyright, Designs and Patents Act 1988
to be identified as the author of this work

ISBN
978-1-84396-654-8
Also available as a Kindle ebook
ISBN 978-1-84396-640-1

A catalogue record for this book is available
from the British Library and the American Library of
Congress. No part of this book may be copied or
reproduced in any form without the consent
of the publisher

Typesetting and pre-press production
eBook Versions
27 Old Gloucester Street
London WC1N 3AX
www.ebookversions.com

Other books by Joan Lock

NON-FICTION

Lady Policeman
The British Policewoman: Her Story
Scotland Yard's First Cases
Scotland Yard Casebook
Tales from Bow Street
Blue Murder?
The Princess Alice Disaster
Dreadful Deeds and Awful Murders

FICTION

Dead Centre
Dead Image
Dead Born
Dead Letters
Dead Loss
Dead Fall
Dead End
Death in Perspective

THE
REAL GOLDEN AGE
OF MURDER

Pistols, Bombs and Motor Bandits

JOAN LOCK

ROBIN BOOKS

Contents

1
The Birth of a Genre

The Golden Age of Detective Stories began with a sisterly bet when her sister Madge warned Agatha that they were difficult to write and when a forty-year-old Irish Railway engineer became bored during a long illness and began to write.[1] Working in a hospital pharmacy gave Agatha the time to consider her plot and inspiration for the murder method came from the poisons on its shelves[2] whilst engineer Freeman Wills Crofts pondered his travel experience to plan the route for *The Cask*. His wife liked his first chapter and showed it to a friendly and helpful neighbour. When Crofts wrote a new third part W Collins also liked the book and published it.[3]

When deciding on her detective Agatha wanted someone different then remembered the colony of Belgian refugees who lived locally and settled on a retired Belgian police detective. For the setting, a large country house such as the one in which she lived. Her plot was ingenious, much of it being disclosed in conversation between the excitable Belgian Detective Poirot, and his companion Hastings, who acted as a kind of butt or stooge.

So, what *kind* of murder did Agatha want? Not an *unusual*

one with an *unusual* motive. It had to be an *obvious* one, such as a husband murdering his wife. But at the same time a reader would think that he could not *possibly* have done it. Although, *of course*, he had.

Madge's battered old typewriter came in useful for producing the first draft but Agatha became tired of trying to compose her epic during her spare time so her mother suggested that a fortnight alone in a hotel might help her concentrate, as it did. And so, gradual tinkering completed, *The Mysterious Affair at Styles,* which was sent off to the publisher, Hodder and Stoughton, who promptly sent it back. More rejections followed but, eventually, the book was accepted by John Lane.

By then, Agatha had forgotten all about it. John Lane had kept the book for so long and, in any case, she had moved from Torquay to London to be with her new husband who had just been demobbed, and had given birth to baby Rosalind. The couple had acquired a flat, a servant to look after it and the nursemaid necessary to take care of Rosalind. And now Agatha had a contract with a clause obliging her to offer them her next five books.[4]

John Lane certainly gave her book a good launch accompanying review copies with the story of Agatha making a bet that, although never having written a detective story before, she could produce one which, while letting the reader have access to all the clues available to the detective, they would *not* spot the murderer. It was a tempting challenge for reviewers to take up and many did so.

Ralph Strauss in *The Bystander* thought that she had 'won it easily' and noted how the reader was diverted from one suspect to another and recommended readers obtained 'Miss Christie's cunning book and spend an exciting two hours'. *The Scotsman* found her puzzle ingenious and that her Belgian detective had methods and ideas which Sherlock Holmes might have been proud to own, whilst *The Yorkshire Post*, agreeing that she had won the bet, added the rider 'but with the aid of plentiful Red Herrings'. True, they were cleverly employed, but they *did* give it a somewhat artificial character.

The Mysterious Affair at Styles sold around two thousand copies and was serialised in *The Weekly Times* – all of which her publisher assured her was not bad for a new author. When announcing that the first chapter would appear in *The Sunday Mercury and News,* John Lane confidently declared the work, 'The Most enthralling Detective Story of the Year' and, in an advertisement in *The Sphere*, quoted an almost orgasmic review from *The British Weekly* which declared that *The Mysterious Affair at Styles* would 'rejoice the heart of all those who truly relish detective stories . . . the feat was amazing . . . the book is put together so deftly that I can remember no recent book of the kind which approaches it in merit: well written, well-proportioned and full of surprises.'

Altogether a splendid launch with perhaps a touch of overkill. However, the financial rewards were insufficient to encourage Agatha Christie to contemplate a career as a writer although husband Archie pointed out that she would receive *more* with each book and encouraged her to write another.[5]

Similarly to Christie's first novel, in Crofts novel the crime was committed by a suspect who turns out to have an unbreakable alibi but then, eventually, doesn't. We follow the mysterious Cask, retracing its movements via the timetables and witnesses from shipping businesses in Paris and London.

His primary detective, Inspector Burnley of Scotland Yard, is experienced, astute and professional - but given to a lot of pondering. Again, as with Christie, there is a clever foreign police detective, Lafarge, this time French. With Burnley he solves the case while the story moves to Paris then back to London and various other venues.

The Scotsman thought *The Cask* 'a bewilderingly intricate puzzle' whilst *The Aberdeen Press and Journal* noted 'Not a page is allowed to become dull, not a chapter is lacking in incident or ingenious contrivance.' Although any reader with much practice in reading mystery stories would have come to the right solution long before the end of the first half, that in no way detracted from 'the thrill of a story surcharged with incident, horror, and keen detective acumen'. The book was highly successful and well outdid *The Mysterious Affair at Styles*.

As the reviews were emerging, Wills Crofts had another book published, *The Ponson Case*, which *The Yorkshire Post* declared a supremely good example of its type. There was no weak place in the construction and everything had been cleared up by patient research of Scotland Yard in 'this ably engineered story', whilst the *Aberdeen Press and Journal* noted, 'Mr Crofts has not made the mistake of presenting the detective as a super mind neither does he represent New Scotland Yard as inhabited by fools'. He was certainly unusual in that!

Meanwhile the genuine Scotland Yard detectives were preoccupied by matters other than country house murders and foreign detectives. Problems such as the easy availability of drugs and guns in post-war London; Fenians suspected to be once again planning to plant their bombs around the capital;

the intentions of 'our own Communists'[6] and, most urgently, the new Motor Bandits.

NOTES FOR CHAPTER 1

1. *Agatha Christie An Autobiography*, p217; Wikipedia: Freeman Wills Crofts: Writing Career
2. *Ibid* p261
3. Wikipedia: Freeman Wills Crofts: Writing Career
4. *Ibid* p283-5
5. *Ibid* p288
6. As the Press dubbed The Communist Party of Great Britain

2
Reality

The Times of the 26th of January 1920 knew the reasons for the current crime wave. They were 'the release from the army and return to their old life of a large number of professional criminals; the failure, or disinclination, of a certain proportion of the discharged soldiers to obtain work; the familiarity with bloodshed and the decreased regard for the sacredness of human life . . . and the unhealthy influence, especially upon youths, of the more sensational and melodramatic cinema films in which crimes of violence are a prominent feature.'

Of course, all this was aided by the current proliferation of guns and drugs but, most of all, by the increased availability of motor cars.

Mass production skills, developed during the war for military purposes, were now available for the production of the motor cars which criminals were suddenly acquiring by buying or stealing them. Without risk of pursuit, they could rob banks and post offices; commit smash and grab raids and handbag snatches; attack bookies at race courses and indulge in inter-gang battles armed with razors and other weapons.

For the sad fact was that the police, who were expected

to catch all these mobile criminals, had no motor vehicles whatsoever apart from a few cars which had been allocated to Divisional Superintendents to replace their dog carts, so they could get about their patches more quickly, and a few motor bikes allotted to Detective Inspectors on the outer districts. Thus, the awkward 1920 *Times* sub-heading, *Police Motor-Cyclist's Burglar Chase*, when one of these mobilised detectives managed to latch onto thieves who were just leaving a house they had burgled out in Bromley and catch them up at Catford.[1] The rest of the Metropolitan Police had no motorised means of mobility.

Earlier in the century, after introducing the Henry system of fingerprint classification which had immensely improved the usefulness of the aid, Scotland Yard had acquired worldwide recognition. Since then, they had not exactly moved with the times. Indeed, they had been amongst the last of the UK police to install telephones worried that if they did so the public would waste their time by constantly ringing up. Cost was also a factor. Huge national spending cuts were being made to public services. Nonetheless, Scotland Yard became aware that *something must* be done about the motor bandits – and the guns.

The murderous year of 1920 had opened in January with the brutal murder of a Chelsea pub landlady the motive for which was so far obscure[2]. However, many current murders tended to be domestic and so required few feats of investigation although the current availability of guns did add variety to the husband/wife murders even leading to two public domestic shoot-outs.

The first of these took place on Monday, 21st June in

The Bell Public House just off Oxford Street when, in a fit of jealousy, Daniel Kildare, 'a coloured musician' shot dead the licensee (who was his wife), her sister, and then himself.[3]

The second occurred on the Wednesday, 23rd of June in the Westbourne Hotel when mining engineer, Edwin Charles Semmens, shot his wife in the eye. She was French, they had met in Paris when he was a Lieutenant in the Canadian Engineers. He had returned to Vancouver to be demobbed, then gone to Nigeria on a work assignment. Returning to London to visit his wife he became suspicious of her relationship with a fellow hotel guest, Major Ditcham. In fact, she left Semmens for the Major, but returned to collect her belongings whereupon Semmens took out a revolver and shot her in the head later telling a friend, 'I have spoiled her beauty.'

He explained to Divisional Detective Inspector Savage that he had been so *upset* that he hadn't known what he was doing. When Caroline died he was charged with murder but the Brixton prison doctor gave evidence that Semmens had been so weak and shaky when admitted that it wouldn't have taken *much* to send him over the borderline as far as his reason was concerned. Another 'expert' declared that he still had traces of malarial poison in his system. The all-male jury found Semmens Not Guilty of either murder or GBH as, clearly, he had not *meant* to kill her. It was, as *The Times* said, quoting the judge, 'A JURY'S REMARKABLE FINDING'[4].

This was to illustrate another problem faced by the police detectives – that of obtaining convictions for murder particularly as such a conviction meant a death sentence for which, it appeared, juries appeared not to want to be responsible - particularly when it applied to members of their own sex who had murdered their wives. However, there was *some* light on the horizon for women in this respect.

As from September, 1920, the risibly—titled *Sex Disqualification (Removal) Act 1919* allowed for women to become eligible to sit on juries although imagined 'problems' with this were soon being thrown up. No doubt, exclaimed *The Times*, 'in a case where a dispute arises as to the fit of a dress or other garment in a Breach of Promise case the judge might welcome the presence of women experts', but it would seem to be repugnant to all proper feeling that the class of evidence which frequently has to be given in the Divorce and Criminal Courts should be discussed by a jury composed of both sexes.[5] Perhaps there should be a male jury and a female jury? And what about when the jury sometimes had to be locked up for the night? What then? 'one can imagine how the ladies would look on the third or fourth days without their ladies maids and toilet requisites'.[6]

Despite these drawbacks one or two women did begin to appear on juries and not all wife murderers received quite such 'remarkable findings' about their cases despite attempts by them and their defence counsels. Engineer Arthur Andrew Clement Goslet, the defendant in the much-publicised *Golders Green Murder* of June, 1920, had the familiar claims of not knowing what he was doing rejected when he admitted actually having taken his wife to the River Brent, struck her on the head with a tyre-lever and thrown her body into the water. According to his defence his lack of awareness while doing all this was due to his having consumed around twenty drinks and having been in an air crash in Germany in 1913 which had rendered him unconscious for a day and a half. He had confessed to killing his wife whilst blaming Daisy Holt, (whom he had bigamously married) for making him do it, in the hope *he* would not be found guilty.

Superintendent Neil told the court that there was no truth in the allegations against Daisy – which she denied. A 'mental expert' *did* declare Goslet insane but Brixton Prison's medical officer was not to proving so helpful on this occasion insisting that he had seen no signs of insanity. Goslet was Found Guilty and sentenced to death.[7]

Of course, the proliferation of guns also made life more dangerous for police officers and security guards. Thirty-four-year-old Metropolitan PC James Kelly was on night duty on 11 February, 1920, in a select residential area of Acton when he approached a man who was acting suspiciously. The man shot him three times; in the chest, left leg and abdomen. On hearing the shots a security guard in the drive of a nearby Rothschild estate ran into the lane where he met a running man dressed as a soldier wearing 'a superior khaki overcoat'. He struck the man in the chest and, in turn, was shot in the chest.

PC Kelly died eleven days later. 'No arrests have yet been made', D I Smith told the Coroner on 24 February, 1920, but enquiries were continuing. Pliers and a screwdriver had been found nearby, it was believed that the gun was automatic and a tall man wearing a short khaki overcoat had got onto the staff underground train of the District Railway at nearby Chiswick Park. A man in a khaki overcoat – now he should be easy enough to find in a London awash with ex-servicemen?[8]

As for the detectives expected to solve these real crimes hopes were pinned on recent changes in CID structure. Up until the previous year each division had had its own Divisional

Detective Inspectors answerable to the Division's uniform Superintendent but the problem had been that the Divisional Detective Inspectors tended to see things only in terms of their own divisions. There was not enough overlap or co-operation between them and this benefited the criminals as did having the uniformed Superintendent in charge of the local CID.

Now, following a suggestion by Chief Inspectors Frederick Wensley and Francis Carlin, there were four Area Superintendents in charge of the divisional CID: Frederick Wensley, Albert Hawkins, Arthur Neil and Francis Carlin, whom the Press dubbed 'The Big Four'. Each had control of a quarter of the Met's CID area and they could make sure that the divisions acted in unison when necessary.

The most influential of these men was the blunt and much-respected Frederick Porter Wensley who now had charge of the CID in all the divisions east of the City as well as E Division (Bow Street) and Thames Division. Like Agatha Christie, Wensley hailed from the West country, although from the more rural county of Somerset where he had been employed as a gardener. His early police service had seen him patrolling the violent streets of London's East End with strips of bicycle tyres nailed to the soles of his boots to deaden their sound so as not to alert Jack the Ripper to his presence. During the 1909, Siege of Sydney Street, he had been trapped on a roof protecting a wounded fellow officer later commenting dryly that he hadn't realised how exciting the Siege had been until he read about it in the newspapers.

Wensley was of the opinion that murders happened more frequently in novels than in real life. His steady climb through the ranks saw him handle many difficult cases but he stuck to the East End only agreeing to go the Scotland Yard to replace his good friend, Detective Chief Inspector Alfred Ward, who had been killed in a Zeppelin raid during the war.

William Rawlings, who worked in the CID central offices in Scotland Yard gave pen pictures of the Big Four of whom, he wrote, 'you could hardly have met four men who were so different from one another'. All had their nicknames.

'Wensley was 'the weasel' ' which probably came, Rawlings surmised, from the Jewish inhabitants of the East End where he had spent most of his service. They called him Mr Vensil or Mr Veasel. 'And he looked like a weasel, too: thin, angular, very Jewish in appearance with bright piercing eyes that bored into you, slow and hesitant in his speech. No one knew as much about the East End as he did.'[9]

True crime writer George Dilnot found that Wensley was 'not a talkative man. He speaks with blunt vigour and stops when he is finished. And his mind works in something of this direct fashion. He goes straight to the heart of the matter' and his detectives knew that he could not be bluffed if they fell short.[10]

Rawlings dubbed Albert Hawkins *Bouncing Albert*. 'He was stoutly built, portly even; but his size did not affect his agility. His manner was hearty; he had a fine sense of humour and kind eyes, quick to light up. He was always smiling.'[11] Hawkin's promotion in the CID had been rapid and, when its area was divided into four, he was given South East London stretching from Piccadilly to Kingston on Thames.

Francis Carlin was a Londoner, born to a Police Constable father in Kentish Town and had joined back in 1890 defying his father who had wanted better for him than the police which was a harder life then.

'*Cocky Carlin* was the shortest man of the four. He was dapper in appearance and always immaculately dressed. Everything about him was quick: his movements, his way of speaking; behind hard eyes there was a quick, calculating mind.'[12]

Carlin got the West End but, as a Divisional D I, he first had to do duty amongst 'the low cut-throat haunts of Southwark and Lambeth with the dark, evil-smelling, alleys, in which crimes were committed nightly' before leaving for 'the glittering atmosphere of the West End with its debonair cultured crooks, who wore spotless linen in place of woollen mufflers.'[13]

In contrast, came the fourth of the Big Four: Arthur Neil. 'Neil had a drooping face and a serious expression. You could never tell what he was thinking and he was slow to smile. He had drooping shoulders. Everything about him was drooping. Inevitably we called him 'Drooper Neil'.[14]

He may have had reason to droop considering the cases he had had to deal with. He found the body of the first Ripper victim; handled the Camden Town Murder in 1907 and the Brides in the Bath case in 1915. For the latter he had carried out the famous demonstration of how the women were drowned 'with a nurse (in a bathing costume)' and was commended by the judge for the way in which he had carried out the investigation.[15] Now, Drooper Neil had charge of the North London CID.

'Of course, our use of such nicknames was an expression of our hero worship.' Rawlings assured his readers. 'It was the homage paid by the novice to the expert.'[16]

A move to make the police more able to protect themselves

against firearms was taken in December 1920 when the Met purchased three hundred new pistols and another eight hundred the following year but the attitude towards their maintenance and whereabouts was somewhat blasé . One P.C. recalled being sent to guard a building with a loaded Webley pistol which he had no idea how to use.[17]

The Big Four realised that some sort of motorised mobility was urgent. In 1919, an experiment with a roving horse-drawn ex-railway van with holes cut in the sides had proved successful. Therefore they now acquired two large motorised Crossley tenders from the demobilised Royal Flying Corps and manned them with two drivers, four inspectors, four sergeants and eight constables – all selected for their knowledge of the haunts and habits of criminals.[18]

Kentish-born Chief Inspector Walter Hambrook, was given charge of the new squad. Like Wensley, he described himself as being of 'yeoman stock' but he had always wanted to be a policeman so, after leaving school aged 13, had left his Kentish village to live in London with friends of the family. There he spent most of his time learning about the Metropolitan Police. Whenever possible, he proudly accompanied his police officer brother on his beat filling in time until he was old enough to join. He did so, aged 21, in 1898[19] and due to his keen attitude and record of crime arrests quickly became a Detective Constable and then a Divisional Detective Inspector.

Hambrook was to claim instant success for his new mobilised squad as they roamed around London seeking out suspicious activity. Quickly dubbed 'the Flying Squad', by a crime journalist with the unlikely name of G T Crook, their battles royal with the gangs of crooks caught the public imagination. Even *The*

Times was drawn into the excitement heading the description of the squad's fight with, and capture of, seven 'alleged burglars' in their van: A NIGHT AFFRAY: SMART POLICE CAPTURE. They reported that Hambrook had been 'savagely kicked' by suspects shouting 'Kill the bastards!' but that his assailant was 'felled to the ground by a blow to the head'.[20]

One senses that Wensley found Hambrook's gung-ho *Boy's Own* attitude irritating – referring, for example, to some criminals as 'bandits'. 'The Flying squad catches thieves because it *knows* thieves', Wensley insisted. 'It's value lies in its mobility.' It was *not* some magic new formula.[21] But he did concede that the motor car had facilitated the operations of the criminals much more than that of the police and thought that, another way to even up the odds would be, when sentencing 'rogues of this type', would be to prohibit them from holding a motor driver's licence after release - except with police permission. [22]

But the problem of the reluctance of juries to convict for murder remained. In March, 1921, Detective Sergeant Woods and DS Heath recognised two wanted men in a Chelsea pub, followed them out, and arrested them. One of them, twenty-year-old 'cinema actor' Douglas Barrington, broke free and ran, as he did so pulling a revolver from his pocket. Sergeant Woods shouted 'Stop him!' and 64-year-old porter, Edwin Payne, who was chatting to a woman nearby, responded by flinging out his arm. Barrington shot him dead, fired again, at DS Woods, then jumped over a hoarding and escaped.

Tracked down via the underworld who did not want trouble, Barrington woke up to find four pistols pointing at him, one from each corner of his bed. His story was, that the revolver had belonged to his friend who found it too big for his pocket so he had been looking after it for him. He had pulled it out to throw it away but had 'lost his head'. He had only intended to frighten the porter and to fire over DS Wood's head.

His counsel cooked up a defence that the porter had no right to stop him as the police had no arrest warrant. But the judge pointed out that he was stopping a man who was armed, so under the Firearms Act, the police had every right to arrest him without warrant and a Murder verdict would be appropriate. Nonetheless, the jury found him Guilty only of Manslaughter of the porter and Not Guilty of the Attempted Murder of DS Woods. When sentencing the judge took into consideration the prisoner's youth giving Barrington only 7 years penal servitude.[23]

NOTES FOR CHAPTER TWO

1. *The Times*, 7 August, 1920
2. *Ibid,* 19 January, 1920; 21 January, 1920
3. *Ibid,* 24 June, 1920
4. *Ibid,* 24 & 28 July, 1920; 30 June & 2 July, 1920
5. *Ibid,* 18 February, 1920 & 23 June, 1920
6. *Ibid,* 25 June, 1920
7. *Ibid,* 4, 7 & 15, May 1920; 23 June 1920; 13 July 1920
8. *Ibid,* 12 & 13 February, 1920; 25 March, 1920
9. *A Case for the Yard,* p53-4
10. *Triumphs of Detection*, p201
11. *A Case for the Yard,* p53-4
12. *Ibid*
13. *Reminiscences of An Ex-detective,* p15
14. *A Case for the Yard,* p53-4

15. *Murders of the Black Museum,* p209
16. *A Case for the Yard,* p54
17. *The Official Encyclopedia of Scotland Yard,* p88
18. *Hambrook of the Yard,* p184
19. *Ibid,* p19-27
20. *The Times,* 20 September 1920
21. *Detective Days,* p190
22. *Ibid,* p192-4
23. *The Times,* March to May 1921

3

Calling in the Yard

Not *all* of the detective story writers famous in the Golden Age were debut novelists nor have they all remained well known since. One such, was J S Fletcher who wrote no fewer than 230 books on a wide variety of subjects, fiction and non-fiction. *The Middle Temple Murder* was published at the same time as Agatha Christie's first, and was regarded as one of his best of (90) detective works, and it was much approved by President Woodrow Wilson.[1]

However, as Joseph Smith Fletcher was born back in 1863 and, as most of his detective works predated the Golden Age and did not 'conform to the closed form and strict rules professed, if not unfailingly observed', some did feel that he was *not* a genuine Golden Ager[2].

Such a dismissal was not the fate of the popular R Austin Freeman who, in 1922, was re-emerging after a lull due to war service as a captain in the Royal Army Medical Corps. He was a doctor, as was his fictional medical-legal investigator Dr Thorndyke

In 1922, whilst one of his short stories was appearing in every issue of the monthly *Pearsons Magazine*[3] alongside

appreciative notes such as: 'another of his fine detective stories'.
. . . 'an exceedingly clever and intensely interesting detective
story', his first new detective novel, *Helen Vardon's Confession,*
was published. The said Helen overhears an argument between
her father and a man named Otway who is suggesting marriage
to her in exchange for his silence about some missing trust
funds and Dr Thorndyke is left to piece together this tale of
blackmail, fraud and death. Not so appreciative of this novel
was this review in *The Daily Herald* by C Edward Morris:

'An improbable love story, mawkish enough in sentiment
to make a cynic of a sighing housemaid, utterly damns R
Austin Freeman's latest thriller *Helen Vardon's Confession.*
The characters in the book are, without exception, slightly
less human than the wax figures in shop windows. The reader
consequently remains as indifferent to the fates of hero and
heroine as he would be to the ultimate disposal of a set of
broken chess men. Will the writers who flood the bookstalls
with mystery and detective stories never realise that ingenuity
of plot alone cannot make their tales readable?'[4]

So, an attack on both the writer and the genre. But this was
not so surprising. *The Daily Herald* was a left-wing newspaper
with strong ties with Russia and Freeman was politically
conservative and let people know. His recent work, *Social Decay
and Regeneration,* had referred to the recent revolution as 'the
Russian catastrophe', and said that society needed protection
from 'degenerates of the destructive or "Bolshevik" type'.[5] He
supported eugenics and attacked the British Labour party.

Later opinions of his detective stories were mixed. In
Bloody Murder Julian Symons likened reading Freeman's
novels to 'very much like chewing dry straw' and thought them

markedly inferior to his short stories, but Raymond Chandler admired him calling him 'a wonderful performer', liked his 'even suspense' and thought there was 'even a gaslight charm about his Victorian love affairs'.[6]

While many of the current London murders in 1920 may lack the need for the exercise of the little grey cells the Yard men still had some complex cases to deal with on unfamiliar ground in the Provinces. If police forces were too small or too ill-equipped or experienced to cope with a murder enquiry themselves they called in The Yard.

This practice of 'calling in The Yard' had gone on since the very early days of the Met's existence. Indeed, since before many counties even *had* police forces of their own. However, in 1907 the Home Office decided that the system should be made more official and streamlined. In consequence, a set number of detective officers at the Central Offices were specially designated for the task on a rota system. They became known as The Murder Squad and were later equipped with a Murder Bag the contents being those which experience had proved most likely to be needed.

To be called away from hot and sooty London to the elegant seaside resort of Eastbourne in August to work on what would become known as *The Beach Murder* may seem as if it promised to be a pleasant change. However, the body of 17-year-old London typist, Irene Munro, had been found in The Crumbles – which was a long, desolate stretch of pebble-covered ground with patches of scrubby grass.

What's more, Superintendent Willard of the East Sussex County force had already taken charge of the case and a senior detective and an inspector from Eastbourne's own city force were also on the scene when Chief Inspector Mercer from Scotland Yard arrived.

Such entanglements could make for dissension and local cooperation was essential. Fortunately, Mercer was gentlemanly and popular and soon took charge. (He was known at the Yard as 'the music maker' due to his indecipherable handwriting. 'You don't read it, Bill', a colleague had commented, 'You turn it upside down and play it on the piano.')[7]

About 25 years earlier Mercer's 'zeal and ability' in tracking down a burglar who had climbed up the front of the house of a Mrs Tyler, strangled her, and got away with a great deal of jewellery, had fast-tracked him into the CID. Since then, he had become known for his unflagging energy while in pursuit.[8]

Irene Munro, The Crumbles victim, lived in South Kensington with her mother who was employed there as a housekeeper but she had been unable to get sufficient time away from her own job as a typist when her mother had gone on holiday to Scotland so Irene had come to Eastbourne on her own for a few days. Her body was found buried in shingle on the beach, with a large blood-stained stone close by. It was established that she had been last seen walking with two quite tall, hatless, young men wearing grey suits of a herringbone pattern and Mercer was soon interviewing a couple of possible suspects but, so far, there was little solid evidence with which to proceed.

Soon, the *Special Correspondent* of *The Times* began producing quite lengthy daily detailed reports on the investigation, which almost gave the impression that *he* was one of the investigation team. Indeed, in the reports he actually admitted questioning some of the witnesses.

He reported, that the victim had been quiet, intelligent and well-educated. She had a French boyfriend with a dark complexion with whom she went on motor car jaunts; the position of her body suggested attempted 'outrage' and the weapon was probably a brick found nearby.

The truth was that Mercer had given several Press briefings asking for their help and soon there had soon been a myriad of suspects and clues: two soldiers seen running across the dunes; a motor car hovering near the murder scene; a man in a tea-room talking to a clearly frightened young woman; a bloody handkerchief found on the Downs – and so on. What now might be termed a media frenzy had resulted and recourse to a clairvoyant was even suggested so that 'a satisfactory reconciliation between the number of apparently contrary facts' might be arrived at.

However, the focus soon reverted to the two hatless young men in grey suits who turned out to be unemployed ex-servicemen Jack Alfred Field and William Thomas Gray who were duly arrested and charged with the murder.

Both denied the charge although, whilst in prison on remand, Gray attempted to fake an alibi with the aid of two fellow prisoners and admitted to one of them that he *had* been with the girl almost up until the hour she died 'but they can't prove it'. When it came to the medical evidence all women were ordered out of court – a practice the suffragettes and early women police had attempted to thwart in London. It was supposedly meant to shield women from witnessing crudity but it often left victims of rape and other sexual offences marooned in a sea of hostile men anxious to prove that they were lying.

Indeed, one magistrate had admitted he did it to save poor men the embarrassment of seeing women listening to this sort of thing.

In this case, the doctor who had been called to the scene told of Irene's three injuries to the lower jaw, which he did not think could have been caused by the heavy stone, but if it had been dropped on the right hand side it might have been what had broken her jaw.

On the other hand, a blow to the under jaw was probably what knocked out two teeth and broke two teeth inwards. The clothing was merely 'drawn up and disarranged' but that could have just happened when they were burying her.

One mystery *was* solved at the trial when Sir Edward Marshal Hall, appearing for the defence of Field, said to Chief Inspector Mercer, 'Please understand I am not suggesting any impropriety, but for your own purpose you thought it best to give certain information to the Press?'

'Yes.'

'And did you find that the newspapers considerably embroidered your information to them?'

'That is so.'

'You followed up a number of alleged clues?'

'I did. A good many.'

Mercer went on to agree that he followed up the ones about the two alleged soldiers (Indeed he had obtained assistance from the Lt Col Deputy Provost Marshal but that lead proved fruitless.) 'They had been three quarters of a mile away from where the body had been found.' And, yes, the one about the frightened girl with the man in the tea-shop – 'There was nothing in it.' And, also, yes, he had had a photograph of the girl published in the *Daily Mail* and flashed onto three cinema screens.

Clearly Mercer had been utilising every current publicity avenue and Defence Counsel Marshall Hall was obviously eager to point to those *other* suspects. But his efforts were in vain. So many witnesses had seen the accused with the girl and eventually the men blamed each other. Field said that he had left Gray with the girl and when he saw him afterwards he told him that he had hit her and covered her with shingle. Gray swore that Field confessed to him that he had knocked the girl unconscious and gone back to strike the final blow. They constantly changed their stories and involved other people in them getting them to lie for them. Eventually, both men blamed each other for the murder and the motive was never established. Was it for her small amount of money and jewels (barmaids gave evidence that the suspects had begun smoking Abdulla cigarettes and drinking Guinness and Bass when they usually smoked Players and drunk bitter) or had they attempted to 'outrage' her and had she resisted?

It *was* established that her death was probably due to the heavy stone being dropped on her head. She had *not* been raped or 'outraged' but was not virgo intacta and there were hints that she had not been averse to making the acquaintance of older men – whatever that implied.

Both men were found Guilty but Appealed. Their Appeals were dismissed.

D I Cherrill, the Yard's fingerprint expert, normally followed the Murder Squad detectives with his large camera and equipment. But his expertise would have been wasted in the case of the murder of a Mrs Seabrook, an elderly widow attacked in her cottage in Redbourne, Hertfordshire, in January, 1921. Local police had allowed kindly neighbours to clean up the scene and wipe all that nasty blood and mess away including that which had appeared on one of the weapons which had caused twenty-eight wounds.

Only recently the Commissioner had declared that he believed that the county and other constabularies would get a good deal of help from our assistance if they asked for it *sooner* than is the case sometimes.

Now, further messages were sent out saying in effect, PLEASE call us in STRAIGHT AWAY and PLEASE leave the crime scene UNTOUCHED!

Despite the misbegotten clean up, the Yard's DI Crutchet got his man – or rather his thirteen-year-old boy, Donald Litton, who lived next door. They found bootmarks outside her cottage, made plaster castes of them and found they matched those of the boy. The boy confessed and explained.

He had wanted to go to the Zoo with his schoolfriends but they had to pay seven shillings to the schoolmaster who was taking them and he had no money. He broke into Mrs Seabrook's cottage where she was sleeping but he found no money by her bed (some had been going missing lately) and, he said, she had woken up and he was frightened so he had hit her with a hammer he had conveniently taken with him. Then he dashed out to bury the hammer in the garden and went back, picked up the poker, and struck her with that causing in total more than 23 scalp wounds of varying degrees and a fractured left forearm and hand. Then he had gone out and tried, but failed, to drown himself in the well in the garden.

He was found Guilty of the murder of the elderly widow and sentenced to be Detained During His Majesty's Pleasure.

Of course officers called in to assist other forces had not only to be prepared for occasional feeling of resentment from the local police officers but suspicion and even obstruction from the local populace. A rather extreme example – with a tragic outcome, took place in the mining community of Abertillery in Monmouthshire, South Wales, in February, 1921.

Nine-year-old Elfreda Burnell had been found dead in a lane with blunt force traumas to the head and a knotted cord tied tightly around her neck. Her elbows had been bound together behind her; her ankles knotted together and she had clearly been subject to attempted rape.

Sent down to investigate was Detective Chief Inspector Harry Helden , who was known as Dutch Harry due to his early police experiences on Thames Division where he specialised in catching out the crew members of the Dutch ships who were especially prone to smuggling and hoodwinking Customs and Excise.

At first it was thought that the attack on Elfreda must have taken place in a shed at the foot of the nearby mountains but doubt set in when it was realised that the body would have had to be carried across a piece of waste land outside the shed – in full view of a long street of houses. However, DI Soden, Helden's second in command, found a handkerchief in the shed which was identified as belonging to the child and witnesses claimed to having heard muffled screams coming from the shed.

On the day she died the girl had been sent to buy poultry food from a shop in which fifteen-year-old Harold Jones had been serving and he had a key to the shed. At the inquest his statements proved inconsistent. Helden was convinced that *this* was their suspect and arrested him. At his trial the shop owner swore Jones had not left the shop that day and his parents insisted that he had not left home that evening so, to the jubilation of the locals, he was found Not Guilty. He attended a celebration meal at which he made a thank you speech to his 'numerous supporters' and was awarded a gold watch.

Alas, seventeen days later Harold Jones lured young Florence Little into his home, strangled her, hit her across the head with a plank of wood and cut her throat. Police held a house to house search and found the girl's body in the Jones's attic. When he was arrested (by the local police) an irate crowd of around 500 strong gathered in protest, demanding his immediate release.

Whilst awaiting trial he confessed to the first killing, giving his motive as 'a desire to kill' but it *was* suggested that the support and attention he received after that first murder may have encouraged him to seek further similar experiences.

Jones served twenty years and was released in 1941 against the recommendations of a psychiatrist. He joined the merchant navy then lived briefly in Newport before moving to Fulham, using the alias Harry Stevens. He died in 1971. In 2018 a BBC documentary argued that Jones was a prime suspect in the unsolved series of London murders committed by a perpetrator known as Jack the Stripper, who is thought to have killed a minimum of six women in the mid-1960s.[9]

The year of 1921 ended in the Murder Squad being called in to a murder so unusual that the elements of the case were to overhang consequent murders in both fact and fiction for some time. Wensley pointed out that murders were either very simple or very difficult to handle. Most people were killed during some emotional crises but, in those which were hard to solve, success often depended on some unhesitating swift stroke which took the culprit unawares. He had known some murderers escape justice because the detective had been too cautious. If a clever criminal knew he was under suspicion and was given time to think and act he would take care that all possible lines of inquiry were blocked and pertinent evidence destroyed.[10]

All that the Home Office and the Director of Public Prosecutions knew in this particular case was that there had been a couple of suspected attempts to poison a young lawyer, Oswald Martin, and that some peculiar instances pointed towards fellow lawyer Herbert Armstrong. Both men practised in Hay-on-Wye, in Brecon Beacons, Wales.

Armstrong was a man of some standing in the community and clerk to the local justices so the affair needed to be handled with some delicacy. The Chief Constable consulted Wensley. He realised that to send one of his detectives down to make *general enquiries* would immediately alert Armstrong who, being a clever lawyer, would instantly cover his tracks. Instead, he sent down the trustworthy and discreet Detective Inspector Crutchet. He was to make *low key* enquiries and then only about those allegations in which there appeared to be some substance against Armstrong and then to go straight to the man himself to enquire whether he cared to give any explanation?

The facts were, that the recently married Mr Martin had received a box of chocolates from an unknown source and, when they had been passed around to some visitors, one of those visitors had become ill and it was found that arsenic had been inserted into the chocolates. Shortly afterwards, Martin had been invited to tea by Armstrong and, imagining this would be to discuss some acute business differences there had been between them, he went. On returning home *he* had become ill and was found to have been poisoned by arsenic. Afterwards, a local doctor had been drawn into a discussion by Armstrong as to *how much* arsenic it would take to kill someone? At the time, he was pressing Martin to come to dinner on New Year's Eve.

Crutchet struck first, descending on Armstrong's office with the Deputy Chief Constable in tow, he put the suspicions to the suspect, and informed him that it was known that he had bought some arsenic some months earlier and asking whether he would like to make a statement?

He did so, denying the accusations but, while he was dealing with one or two 'urgent matters' at his desk, was caught removing a packet containing three-and-three-quarter grains of the poison.

Nor had it gone unnoticed that, after the recent death of Armstrong's wife, her will – which was written in his handwriting but signed by her – had left everything to him and ignored her children.

Her body was duly exhumed and found to contain so much arsenic it polluted the earth round her coffin. He was found Guilty of her murder and was hanged. However, one the chief things people remember about this case are Armstrong's words 'Excuse fingers' which he was reputed to have said as he selected a particular scone to hand to Martin to ensure that he received the poisoned one.

1921 had been a busy year but Wensley was going to have to eat his words about the rarity of real-life murders when 1922 *also* turned out to be poisonous and bloody.

NOTES FOR CHAPTER THREE

1. Whodunit, p159

2: J S Fletcher, Ref 3: Introduction: *Further Rivals of Sherlock Holmes* (Penguin, 1973)

3. Pearsons Magazine: A monthly periodical which first appeared in 1896. Speculative literature, political discussion, and the Arts. Many of famous writers' short stories first published there.

4. Daily Herald, 3 August,1922.

5. Wikipedia: R Austin Freeman, Political Views

6. Bloody Murder, pg87

7. Ibid: Critical Reception

8. A Case for the Yard, p57

9. The Evening Telegraph, 28 April, 1924.

10. The Times, 23, August, 1920 – 19, January, 1921.

11. Wikipedia: Harold Jones (Murderer): References and Cited Works.

12. Harold Jones (Murderer)

13. Detective Days, p259-262

4

The Rules

As the Golden Age of the Detective Story evolved so did the sets of supposed 'rules' as to how they should be written. Amongst the twenty rules dreamed up by various self-appointed legislators were that the chief interest of the story should be mental analysis; that there should be no love interest nor atmospheric pre-occupations to hold up the action and introduce irrelevant issues; that the detective should *never* be the culprit and neither should a servant because this was a too easy a solution and the culprit must be a decidedly worth-while person.[1]

Of course, reality had already produced servant suspects. In fact, back in late Victorian times there was a spate of murders by servants, due either to their simmering resentments about their pay and conditions and/or as a means of theft from their masters and mistresses. Indeed, it was an earlier such murder, that of Lord William Russell in 1840, which had helped bring about the Yard's detective branch in 1842.[2]

However, Lady White, the middle-aged widow of the Chairman of the LCC, probably felt she had shrugged off servant problems, and certainly any threats from them, when she elected to live in a small but select West End Hotel. On 13 March, 1922, she had spent a typically pleasant evening playing bridge with like-minded residents before retiring to her room at 11pm. She did not lock her door. She had never found that necessary.

The following morning, when the chambermaid knocked and entered with hot water for Lady White's morning toilet, she found her unconscious with severe wounds to her head and her pillow soaked with blood.

The first police on the scene were Superintendent Arthur (Drooper) Neil and Divisional Detective Inspector George Cornish. They first concentrated on questioning the staff who were all buzzing with opinions as to who might have committed the crime. The 18-year-old boot boy, Henry Jacoby, even insisted that he had heard some whispering on the stairs that night. The next day Lady White died.

Given the limited access to the hotel it was soon decided that it had been an inside job and police homed in on the boot boy Jacoby who, after one or two statements denying the assault, eventually came clean and admitted that he had gone into Lady White's room to steal money – not jewellery – 'they can't swear to money'. When she woke up and screamed he had taken fright and battered her around the head several times with the hammer he had conveniently taken with him.[3]

The following month came another murder in which the suspect was a young servant but, apart from that, this was a murder unlike any other.

Late on an April day in 1922 in Tonbridge, Kent, 17-year-old footman, Ernest Albert Walker, approached local Constable Sheepwash and asked to be taken to the police station, 'As I have done a murder in London.'

He explained that the body was at 30 Lowndes Square, in Chelsea, and added in typical fashion, 'I don't know what made me do it.'

There was no answer at the Chelsea address, the residents being away and the servants out for the evening, so Divisional D I Hedley broke in.

On the floor of the Butler's Pantry he found a bloodstain and when he opened the door of the butler's bedroom he was greeted by a rush of gas. Lying just under the gas radiator they found a badly-injured messenger boy, 14-year-old Reginald Davis, still wearing his uniform hat, cape and pouch. He was new to the job but had been judged by his superiors to be 'a bright, intelligent fellow'.

It turned out that Walker, the footman, having been left alone in the house, decided to commit suicide, which he had been planning to do since his mother's death. But not wanting to die alone he sent for a messenger boy and wrote out this chilling murder plan:

1) Ring up Sloane Street. 2) Wait at the front door. 3) Invite him in. 4) Bring him downstairs. 5) Ask him to sit down. 6) Hit him on the head (with an iron bar). *7) Put him in the safe. 8) Keep him tied up. 9) Torture. 10) Prepare for the end. 11) Turn on gas. 12) Sit down, close window.*

Of course, things didn't work out exactly as planned. Walker did not die – but the messenger boy did – in hospital the next day.

The Coroner, who clearly felt he knew what had encouraged the footman to act in such a heartless and peculiar manner, asked the Butler, who obviously thought well of the boy, if he read trashy literature?

'I have seen him reading detective novels, but not very often,' he replied and added that as far as he knew Ernest had only been to the pictures twice (of course, he meant the moving pictures).

Later, when the books from the footman's room were produced the Coroner pronounced them 'sensational detective trash'.

Walker's father had already revealed the 'real' reason for the boy's behaviour: 'Two of his uncles had been in lunatic asylums.'

His Counsel, Mr St John Hutchinson, offered a more sophisticated defence: 'epileptic automatism' meaning that the young footman had not really been aware of his actions. He brought an 'expert' to court to agree.[4]

Another matter also came to Walker's aid – the jury were instructed *not* to be influenced by the Press hullabaloo about what had happened to Jacoby the boot boy. He had been sentenced to death with a strong recommendation to mercy due to his age. But his Appeal had been rejected and he was hanged whereas prostitute murderer Ronald True, whose Appeal had also been rejected, was saved from the gallows by the Home Secretary who had three eminent men declare him insane and sent to Broadmoor. It had not been lost on the Public consciousness that True came from a wealthy, influential family, whilst Jacoby did not.

Additional proof of insanity had also been revealed in Jacoby's family and he had a history to setting fire to a house. Wensley, who did not believe in capital punishment for *all* murders because some occurred in the heat of the moment, was *not* sympathetic. He thought that Jacoby 'was just a conceited, consequential, precocious boy who rushed into a murder confident of his own cleverness to evade detection'. He pointed out that Jacoby had not cared about the danger to the people in the house he set fire to.

Nevertheless, *The Times had* reported that the boy had smiled all the way through one of his hearings and the expression on Jacoby's face in one of his Press photographs does hint of some mental lack.

The footman, Walker, was found Guilty but Insane and, like True, sent to Broadmoor.

On 30 November, 1921, Wensley was appointed head of the Central Branch of the CID but continued to retain the control of his old area and 'there were times when I felt justified in taking an active interest in an investigation.' He more or less admits that it was the excitement of the chase which pulled him back in.[5]

One of these investigations was about the murder of a man named Grimshaw who had been found dead in Higham's Park, a lonely part of Epping Forest. He had been killed by violent blows to his head. A man had been seen slinking about in the forest earlier and there was an idea that it might have been Grimshaw being a peeping Tom and that he had been killed by some angry young man who was disturbed when in the heat of passion.

Enquiries about Grimshaw's associates revealed that he had recently been seen in the company of a 22-year-old girl although, lately, *she* had been seen with a young man named Yeldham and it turned out that *he* was the man who had been slinking through the forest.

The girl had connections in Braintree in Essex so Wensley and the Divisional D I Tommy Tanner went down there and discovered that she and Yeldham had been married in the registry office there three days after the murder – and – since wives could not be coerced into testifying against their husbands . . .

The pair were arrested and soon broke down and admitted the killing. Yeldham's story was that he had followed the girl and Grimshaw into the forest and been overcome by jealous passion when the man put his arm around her waist. However, the victim was known to carry a lot of money and the murder turned out to be part of the pair's plot to rob and murder Grimshaw by using his infatuation with the girl to ensnare him.

Wensley described the 23-year-old Yeldham as 'a well-set-up physical specimen of a man, but one of those callous and indifferent types who are so often associated with violent crimes' and the girl to be 'passably good-looking, but with nothing that put her out of the ordinary run of her class'.

Both were convicted and Yeldham was hanged but the girl was reprieved.[6]

One wonders how the divisional detective inspectors felt about Wensley taking such a close interest in their cases? Were they grateful for the benefit of his experience or did they think he was stopping them gaining their own and cramping their style?

It had only been four years since the end of the war which had cost so many lives (including those of both Wensley's sons) so it was natural that memorials large and small continued to be erected. To unveil them such men as Field Marshall Sir Henry

Wilson GCB DSO were much favoured. An Irish Baronet, he had been one of the most senior staff officers during the war and was a man of great charm and ebullience. However, he was thought by some to be too friendly with the French and was unpopular with others for dabbling in the current 'undeclared war' in Northern Ireland.

The memorial unveilings currently listed in his diary were the Roll of Honour to the 749 pupils of the famous public school, Marlborough College, and that at Liverpool Street Railway Station to the men of the Great Eastern Railway who had also fallen. The latter ceremony took place at 1pm on 22 June, 1922 and Wilson, resplendent in full uniform, was back outside his home in Eaton Place, Belgravia, within an hour. Alas, he never made it from cab to door. Two ex-soldiers, both of whom had been wounded when serving at the Front, stepped forward and shot him six times.

Of course, there was no mystery to be solved with this murder. The assassins were Irishmen, Joseph O'Sullivan and Reginald Dunne, who had only decided to carry out the killing the previous evening and had not formed any escape plan. They were chased by (unarmed) police officers and, turning to fire on them, injured two and a chauffeur, but were caught up by a crowd and arrested by other police officers. The fact that O'Sullivan had a wooden leg may well have aided the pursuit.

When the news got out Parliament was adjourned, the Prince of Wales's birthday dinner at Buckingham Palace was postponed and the Yard began investigations as to *who* had *ordered* the killing. Suspected by many was the Irish Free State leader Michael Collins who had referred to Wilson as 'a violent Orange partisan'. But others thought it more probably a lone effort.

(Collins himself was to be assassinated two months later. By then, it was accepted that the killers of the Field Marshal, now themselves executed, had mistakenly believed he was responsible for Catholic deaths in Northern Ireland.)

Lady Wilson attended the Marlborough College unveiling in her late husband's place and presented the two wounded police officers and chauffeur with gold watches. A memorial to Field Marshal Wilson was erected by the Great Eastern Old Comrades Association alongside the one he had unveiled an hour before his death.[7]

This was not London's first current overspill from 'the Irish problem'. On Sunday, April 3rd 1921, a man had been found shot dead on Ashford Manor Golf Links in Middlesex. Beside him was a note saying , 'Let spies and traitors beware.' Signed I.R.A.

The victim of the Golf Links Murder was 21-year-old Vincent Fovargue who had escaped from a police escort in Dublin. Since then he had not kept a very low profile having attended dances held by the Irish Self Determination League in Fulham, telling members that his name was Edward Stanton and that he lived in Chelsea. Seven of those involved in handling the case, including the inquest jurymen, received threatening letters saying there would be bereavements in their families should verdicts of a certain character be returned. So it was unsurprising that, nearly three weeks later, Divisional Detective Inspector Smith told the inquest jury that he had been unable to obtain any further evidence. Consequently, a verdict of Wilful Murder by some person or persons unknown was returned.

The following month masked men broke into a house in Shepherds Bush and shot the occupant, Mr Horace McNeil, in the stomach. His son-in-law was serving with the Royal Irish Constabulary and, reported *The* Times, many people with relatives in the Crown forces in Ireland were receiving threatening letters. McNeil died in hospital. A number of suspects were taken into custody but neither of these crimes were solved.[8]

'Few crimes with which I have been associated aroused greater public interest' wrote Wensley in reference to the case he was called into by K Division's Divisional Detective Inspector Francis Hall on 4 October, 1922. In fact, this was part of Superintendent Neil's patch but he was on leave.

Clearly Wensley thought this was another of those cases which needed him to become more involved. Indeed, he was later grateful that his position had allowed him to utilise and acquire the assistance of the whole force without any time-wasting – one of the reasons why the Big Four had been formed.

He admitted that he initially felt no suspicion about the incoherent woman who had been returning home to Ilford after a visit to the theatre with her husband when he had suddenly staggered, collapsed and died. Later, he was found to have been stabbed several times but she was unable to account for his wounds and, Wensley felt, there was no doubt that her distress was genuine.

'She could scarcely have been called a pretty woman, but she had a distinctly attractive personality.' She also carried herself well, was dressed tastefully and spoke with an air of culture. 'In moments of animation she must have been a woman of considerable fascination.'

She was, of course, twenty-eight-year-old Edith Thompson and her husband was the thirty-two-year-old shipping clerk Percy Thompson. She could find no reason why anyone would want to kill him but when Wensley talked to Percy's brother he mentioned a young man named Bywaters who had been friendly with Edith and had once lodged with them saying, 'I could never understand how he tolerated the situation.' (meaning the husband of course). However, the brother did *not* think Bywaters could have anything to do with the crime as he was away at sea. In fact, he was on leave in England but due to rejoin his ship the following day. Wensley had him tracked down and invited to Ilford Police Station.

He turned out to be 'a stalwart, handsome young fellow of twenty, but both in appearance and in manner he was much older. His attitude, as he greeted us, was full of self-assurance with a kind of studied arrogance in his tone.'

'What do you want with me?' he demanded sharply.

By now the force had twenty policewoman one of whom, Lilian Wyles, was a member of the CID but whose duties were mostly to take statements in cases of sexual assault and to assist the male officers where necessary. Wensley sent for her and told her to go into a room with Mrs Thompson. 'Listen to what she says. Don't say much yourself; keep it to 'yes' and 'no.'

Whilst there with the agitated woman, who was demanding to be allowed to go home, Detective Inspector Hall, two sergeants and Bywaters came out of the CID office and walked slowly past the window. By then, Flying Squad men had been to Bywater's home and found affectionate letters from Edith, some with a sinister undertone. As they passed the window

Mrs Thompson turned away impatiently but later she saw him and exclaimed, 'Not that, not that! No! No! Why did he do it? Oh, God!'[9]

Wensley recalled it slightly differently, 'Oh, God! Oh God!, what can I do? ' she moaned. 'Why did he do it? I did not want him to do it . . . I must tell the truth.' Then she admitted that she had seen him running away after the attack.[10]

More letters from her were found in his box on board ship. These were more sinister. They described her putting broken glass into her husband's food and methods of poisoning him – although no poison was found in his exhumed body.

Both were charged with murder. Her Defence attempted to persuade the jury that she was living in a world of make believe and was merely trying to keep her lover interested. Bywaters did not claim to have been incited to murder indeed he insisted that Mrs Thompson knew nothing about his intentions but both were found Guilty and hanged. Clearly juries had little sympathy for errant females.

There had been much agitation to have her reprieved and some thought that she had been executed for adultery but that, following the furore about True's reprieve, the Home Secretary had been too nervous to save her.

A great deal has been written about the case since but Wensley was of the opinion that much false sentiment had been invoked for 'a cruel and calculated murder in which it was hard to see a redeeming feature'. He thought that she had been fully aware of what was to come on the walk home that evening in Ilford and had delayed shouting for help until Bywaters had escaped and her husband was dead.[11]

There were various other murderous events in this bloody year one of which was the attempt to murder the Commissioner, Brigadier General Horwood, with poisoned chocolates. He was very unpopular with his men whom he had not bothered to get to know. Neither had he made any real attempt to resist a Government demand that their pay should be cut by The Geddes Act. According to one of his clerks he was 'an unattractive man who mistook arrogance for leadership'.[12]

However, he had not been the only target. Similar gifts of poisoned chocolates had been sent to other senior policemen by a paranoid lunatic named Walter Tatum but the Commissioner had been the only one to be foolish enough to sample them. His men were pleased he did so as it enabled them to award him a sarcastic nickname: The Chocolate Soldier.

NOTES FOR CHAPTER FOUR

1. *Bloody Murder*, p102-103

2. *Dreadful Deeds and Awful Murders*, p59-71

3. *Detective Days*, p271; *The Times*, 15 March, 1922–23 May, 1922

4. *The Times*, 24 April, 1922–3 May, 1922; *The British Journal of Psychiatry*, October, 1922.

5. *Detective Days*, p216-217

6. *Ibid* p217-221

7. *Wikipedia:* Sir Henry Wilson, 1st Baronet; *The Times*, 23 June-11, August, 1922

8. *The Times, 28 December, 1922*

9. *A Woman at Scotland Yard*, p147-8

10. *Detective Days*, p222-237

5
1923

Agatha Christie *may* not have gone to school nor gained any educational qualifications[1] but the same could not be said of the next two detective story authors to emerge in 1923: Dorothy L Sayers and GDH Cole both of whom had enjoyed good, formal educations.

Dorothy was the only child of the chaplain of Christchurch Cathedral in Oxford and the headmaster of the choir, who began teaching her Latin when she was six. She went on to the Godolphin School and to win a scholarship to Somerville College to study modern languages and medieval literature. She achieved First Class Honours although, of course, was not *allowed* to graduate *then* because she was a woman.

In 1920 she *did* receive her BA and, at the same time, was awarded an MA. She also began working out the plot of her first detective novel, *Whose Body?* Having already published two volumes of poetry, one of them religious.

By 1923, when the novel was published, she was employed as a copywriter with S H Benson's Advertising Agency, a job at which she rather excelled. *Whose Body?* Introduced an amateur detective, the wealthy, well-educated, Lord Peter Wimsey, a man with a remarkable range of interests and talents as well as being brave and charming. He puts these talents to use by solving the mystery of the body of a naked man being found in a bath wearing nothing but a pair of *pince nez* – a task which Police Inspector Sugg had been employed to do. Wimsey allows him to take credit nonetheless which ends their long enmity.[2]

The Leeds Mercury review, titled *A WOMAN'S DETECTIVE STORY*, declared 'We had hardly thought a *woman* writer would be so robustly gruesome . . . enter a pair of detectives, a professional and an amateur and between them, not forgetting a very wonderful valet, they fill the book with the solution to a very diverting problem.'

The Scotsman found that the detective, Lord Peter Wimsey, was 'worth watching'.

Later, Julian Symons (poet, biographer, crime novelist and critic), whilst admiring Sayers' careful craftsmanship and her clear and incisive mind, admitted that it was not easy to write fairly about her. To her admirers she was the finest of detective story writers but for others her work was long-winded and ludicrously snobbish.[3]

By contrast GDH (George Douglas Howard) Cole, although a product of St Paul's School and Balliol College, Oxford, was very politically involved and known as 'a libertarian socialist'. By 1923, he had already authored several economic and historical works including biographies of radical reformers, William Cobbett and Robert Owen. *The Brooklyn Murders* was Cole's first detective novel but after that he wrote them in tandem with his wife Margaret and they produced one and sometimes two or three more novels a year.

His publisher, Collins, provided a similar debut review peg

to that of Agatha Christie's with Cole loving detective fiction and always wanting to try his hand at it. This worked, in some cases eliciting a definite 'Yes, yes he can!' and some flattering words. However, the *Yorkshire Post & Leeds Intelligencer*, whilst describing 'a most ingenious and baffling plot' went on to rap Cole's knuckles over the fact that he gave away the identity of the murderer too early.

'It is perhaps permissible for a reviewer of fiction to hope that in his writing as an exponent of Guild Socialism Mr Cole is more careful in his development of the theme.'

He then goes on to point out that Cole brings on far too many characters in the first ten or twelve pages of *The Brooklyn Murders,* some of which were quite subordinate to the story, and also that his detective techniques were wanting. 'It is, for example, highly improbable that any intelligible or identifiable fingerprints could be found on a collar or a stone club' and the stone club could hardly inflict such a terrible blow without breaking. Also, the title is misleading – the book has nothing to do with New York. However, 'in spite of major and minor points open to criticism, Mr Cole has written an entertaining book, and gives promise of yet better.'

Again, as with R Austin Freeman's vituperative critique from the *Daily Herald,* one wonders whether there was another reason for this hyper-critical review? Perhaps some disapproval of the author's ideas? Cole *was* vocal about Press ownership and his political pronouncements, such as that he would like to see the complete suppression of advertising, were, as usual, gaining plenty of Press coverage. And, as Martin Edwards points out in *The Golden Age of Murder,* Cole's first book was unusual for its sympathetic portrayal of Trade Union leaders and his refusal to demonise the Bolsheviks who, at the time, were getting a very bad Press in the UK. One does not expect the likes of Cole to present us with another of those unlikely aristocratic detectives but Martin did find his police character, Superintendent Wilson, suffered from a remarkable lack of charisma.[4]

By odd coincidence, at the same time, *The Brooklyn Bank Murders* were featuring in news reports on the *real* murders of two Brooklyn bank messengers.[5]

Meanwhile, Agatha Christie was publishing her third book, *Murder on the Links*, possibly inspired by her husband's devotion to golf, or maybe, also, the 1922, I. R. A. golf links murder. By now, Freeman Wills Crofts was on his fourth publication – the title of which most aptly demonstrated his reputation as a practical man – *The Pit-Prop Syndicate.*

Back in the real crime world 1923 was launched by twenty Sinn Feinn members attempting to set fire to a huge Thameside oil dump (belonging to the Vacuum Oil Company) in Wandsworth. Since it was adjacent to a gas works, a distillery and various other sites stacked with combustible material this could have been disastrous. Fortunately, the police got wind of the plot in time to catch them at it. The Fenians had already managed to bore through twenty-five barrels, insert paraffin-soaked material and set some alight when police whistles alerted them. They tried to escape across the river, some by grabbing a boat or climbing onto a barge.

They fired pistols at two approaching police officers only just missing them. It turned out that their efforts had been in vain anyway. They had chosen the wrong barrels. There were twenty-two grades of oil on the site but, as reported by former DI Kenneth Ferrier, 'They had broached the barrels containing a heavy oil which would have been more likely to put a fire out than start one.'[6]

In court, they freely admitted their guilt and were also charged with the attempted murder of the two constables. The principles were given eight years and the others four years penal servitude each.

Murders often have a sense of *déjà vu* about them not always due to copy-cat crime. One type merely seems to set off others. In the 1920s poisoned chocolates became quite the vogue. They had cropped up the year before the Armstrong case in Yorkshire when farmer Thomas Liddle was found guilty of sending them to eight people who had given evidence opposing him when he was trying to fraudulently pass off a will as that of his late sister. The jury acquitted him of attempt to murder but guilty of intent to endanger life. He was also given five years for fraud and ten for the chocolates.

According to Edward Marjoribanks, Marshall Hall's biographer, it was an earlier poisoned chocolates case which set the famous barrister off on his quest to become a lawyer when his father took the fourteen-year-old Marshall to hear the case of the Brighton Poisoner, Christiana Edmunds. Having failed to kill the wife of her doctor, with whom she had fallen violently in love, to cover herself she began spreading around chocolates laced with strychnine and consequently killed a small boy. She was eventually sent to Broadmoor.

Inevitably, poisoned chocolate were also to find their way into detective fiction as they did in 1929 in *The Poisoned*

Chocolates Case by Anthony Berkeley, which his fictional police were unable to solve so a group of amateurs were challenged to do so.

In February, 1923, came the first of that year's taxicab murders. This was *not* a case requiring much solving, although it was as strange as that in any fiction. Just after midnight a cab drove up to Vine Street Police Station near Piccadilly Circus and a young man, Bernard Pomroy, alighted. He walked into the inspector's office, showed his bloodstained hands and said, 'The women is in the cab.'

Unconscious on the floor of the cab, with wounds to her throat, was Alice Cheshire, a 22-year-old domestic servant. She died in hospital shortly afterwards. She and Pomroy had been 'walking out' for almost four years but, after Alice took a temporary job at West Hampstead, Percy took up with Mabel, her sister, and got her in the family way. That fact had only just been revealed to her mother, whom he informed that he could do nothing about it until he had seen Alice. He had picked up Alice from West Hampstead to take her to the Hippodrome Theatre and, as they were leaving he said to the cook, 'Why not say goodbye properly, in case she does not come back again.' The cook thought he must be joking.

Pomroy admitted the murder, was charged and convicted offering no explanations as to why he had killed his fiancé. When asked why sentence of death should not be passed on him he said 'If I did say anything it would alter my case altogether, therefore I will not.' After sentencing, reported *The Times* 'he smiled and stepped briskly from the dock.'[7]

The second taxi-cab murder was signalled at 2 a.m., on the morning of 10 May, 1923, when Superintendent Carlin received a phone call from Inspector Berrett, one of his most conscientious and hard-working Divisional DIs, to say that a taxi-driver had been found shot dead in Baytree Road, Brixton. Spread beside the victim were a pair of gloves, a flashlight and a revolver, from which three shots had been fired (two remaining in the chamber), a hammer and a gold-knobbed walking stick. Carlin had the descriptions of these items sent to all London police stations and asked the Press to publish them – concentrating on the walking stick.

Next day, he was informed that a man named Eddie, or Vivian or Viv, had been seen in the pubs and cafes of Charing Cross Road carrying such a stick. Viv was a convicted thief known to the police so the hunt was on. He was traced to his girlfriend's home and bearded. He told them a tale of a friend, Scottie Mason, who had written to him from gaol asking him to acquire a revolver. The pair had arranged to do a housebreaking job together but, when Scottie was released, Viv had been sick with a stomach bug so Mason had gone alone – taking with him the revolver and cane – and returned with torn trousers, scraped knees and hands.

When challenged by police, Mason declared that he had received the injuries when trying to get into a house in Norbury – but could not give details. Curious as to what the cab was doing in Baytree Road Carlin organised a house to house there which turned up a woman who recalled that a man had come to her door asking to be let through her house to get to the next street. She picked Scottie out on an identity parade. He was charged with murder and his friend Vivian became chief witness for the Crown revealing a deadly confession he claimed had been made to him by Scottie. Then Scottie insisted that

Vivian had been with him all evening. Nonetheless he was found Guilty and sentenced to death.

Who knows *which* criminal was only trying to save his own skin? However, after what Carlin described as a considerable amount of agitation on Scottie's behalf, the sentence was commuted to one of penal servitude for life. Carlin could not think of a more unnecessary murder. Desperate for cash, Scottie had got only £2 from the dying taxi driver.[8]

NOTES FOR CHAPTER FIVE

1 In her autobiography, p96, Christie supposes that she must have had lessons of some kind and elsewhere records various bouts of tuition.

2. Wikipedia, Dorothy L Sayers: Biography: Detective Fiction: *Whose Body?*

3. Bloody Murder, p108

4. The Golden Age of Murder, p76

5. The Scotsman, 29 November, 1923

6. Crooks and Crime, p199-208

7. The Times, 2 March, 1923

8. Reminiscences of An-Ex-Detective, p101- p112

6

Women in Peril

Interest in Detective fiction first began with a short story, *Murder in the Rue Morgue,* by Edgar Allen Poe, and his subsequent tales between 1841 and 1845. It continued largely due to the popularity of the detective short stories in various magazines.

One of the Golden Agers, H C Bailey, had been writing romantic and historic short stories then, in 1920, began producing detective short story collections. These featured Reggie Fortune, a doctor associated with the Home Office who tackled dark themes such as child abuse and police corruption. Reggie became one of the most popular of the Golden Age detectives and his short stories were admired by Sayers and Christie but, Martin Edwards points out, 'his star has fallen since and his stylistic quirks mean that today his work is an acquired taste'.[1]

As a child in a family of nine children Welshwoman, Ethel Lina White, wrote essays and poems for children's papers, went on to short stories and mainstream novels then, in 1931, tried a crime novel, *Put Out The Light*. Well known in the Golden Age, Ethel's speciality was 'women in jeopardy' which is aptly demonstrated by her short story *Cheese*[2]. In that, an innocent 'fresh from the country' girl manages to help police catch a murderer, while also awakening the feelings of the dour and cautious Inspector Angus Duncan of Scotland Yard. Her novel, *The Wheel Spins* (1936), was filmed by Alfred Hitchcock in 1938 as *The Lady Vanishes* and two years after her death her book, *Some Must Watch,* was made into another highly successful movie, *The Spiral Staircase.*[3]

Conan Doyle was, of course, the short story game changer with his omnipotent Sherlock Holmes whose fame remains world-wide so that even in American TV cop shows you have a detective muttering ruefully, 'Well, I'm no Sherlock.'

In the 1920s the detective short story was still popping up here or there in provincial newspapers such as, *Detective Gripper of Scotland Yard* by Joseph Gilroy, which appeared as OUR SHORT STORY in *The Mid-Sussex Times* on August 24th, 1920. Since it had already appeared in *The Todmorden Advertiser* in July, it was not exactly *theirs.*

In very sharp contrast to the 1923 taxi cab crimes came the most sensational murder of the year – that of the immensely wealthy 22-year-old Egyptian Prince Fahmy Bey. The venue was a luxury suite at the Savoy Hotel in The Strand and the murder occurred at 2 a.m. on the night of 9 July when a great storm hit London. There was no need to search for the killer since she was his French wife Marguerite who was found with the automatic Browning pistol in her hand and with three empty cartridges scattered around her feet.

'What have I done? What will they do to me?' She exclaimed to the night manager. 'Oh, sir, I have been married six months and I have suffered terribly.'

Very oddly, the previous day, when at lunch, the hotel's orchestra leader had asked her if she would like him to play any particular tune. She had replied that, since her husband was going to kill her in twenty-four hours, she was not very anxious for music.

The pair, who had met in Cairo, were clearly not a happy couple having been frequently witnessed have violent rows. She, it seemed, was wilful and had been accustomed to having her own way as a successful, wealthy courtesan. He, a young Muslim, was madly jealous and intent on training her to behave as a wife should.

The night porter kept hold of her, while instructing staff to get a doctor, an ambulance, the General Manager and inform Bow Street police. Her dreadfully injured husband was escorted away.

The first police officer on the scene was a Sergeant George Hall whilst Divisional Detective Inspector Alfred Grosse went first to Charing Cross Hospital, then its mortuary to inspect Ali's body.

The crime was an unusual one but it soon became apparent that's its handling was also to be. The hotel staff had already been able to clean up the scene – something the Met criticised other forces for allowing. Overall charge of the investigation was given to Superintendent Parker of the Special Branch whose responsibilities included Royalty Protection – *possibly* because at first there was the misapprehension that Ali really *was* a Prince. But the anomalies continued: the forensic attention was scanty and there were no photographs of the scene. After Marguerite's brief appearance at Bow Street Magistrate's Court she was allowed to go to Holloway Prison by cab instead of facing the iniquity of a ride in the prison van with the other prisoners.

It was to be many years before the reasons for this unusual treatment were revealed in *The Woman Before Wallace* by Andrew Rose, published in 2013. It told of the passionate affair that Marguerite and Prince Edward had enjoyed during the war when he was a staff officer, behind the lines in France, and she had a good many letters to prove it.

Not only might the British public disapprove of the liaison but also the fact that he had been enjoying a sybaritic lifestyle while his countrymen were enduring the life and death struggle in the trenches and dying in their thousands. True, the Prince *had* wanted to go to the Front but that had not been deemed sensible so he had served as a Staff Officer all the while complaining of the boredom of it all and sometimes being indiscrete in the letters to Marguerite which contained information some of which might have been helpful to the enemy.

When it came to the murder, Marguerite claimed she had been protecting herself, but she *had* fired *three* shots so things *should* have looked bleak for her. However, the famous barrister, Marshall Hall, represented her, painting a dramatic picture of a poor delicate little Western woman suffering at the hands of a cruel Oriental who had perverted sexual appetites as the result of which she suffered from piles and a fistula caused, she claimed, by her husband's persistence in sodomising her and refusing to pay for a subsequent operation.[4]

Curiously, the day after the murder, the Prince of Wales's plans to visit his ranch in Canada were suddenly brought forward. 'It is fortunate that he (the Prince) is off to Canada', wrote the Foreign Secretary Marquess Curzon to Grace Curzon. Earlier, it had been reported in *The Times* that he would be making a Royal visit to Aberystwyth and Winchester at the time he would now be away.

Marguerite was acquitted, although the Egyptian Bar was not as delighted as she, complaining to our Attorney General about Marshall Hall's blanket unfavourable depiction of their countrymen. The author, Andrew Rose, goes so far as to refer to it as 'a Show Trial' and seems to be in no doubt that, having discovered that Ali intended to divorce her, that she had decided to kill him.

After that she devoted much energy into trying to extract as much money as possible from his estate but found Sharia Law did not take too seriously claims from the widow of the man she had killed. She had already tried to pressure Prince Edward with veiled threats regarding his letters and, it seems, that by August 1923, most were back in the hands of the Prince's aides and that *this* may have been what had ensured her acquittal.[5]

But, of course, *most* murders were, as usual, run-of-the-mill killings of women by their partners or ex-partners and juries were ever more reluctant to convict of murder due to the death penalty so tended to go for manslaughter instead, sometimes resulting in even more risible penalties for the perpetrators.

There was a man up at Newcastle Assizes for murder of his wife whose screams had awoken the neighbours. She had been found almost decapitated the following morning. He claimed that she had attacked him, given him wounds to the throat, then cut her own throat. Despite Bernard Spilsbury advising that her wounds could *not* have been self-inflicted the all-male jury found him Not Guilty of murder. (Interestingly, *The Times* report actually made a point of mentioning that the jury was 'all male' and, by now, women were admitted on jurys.[6])

The jury in The Crumbles murder had wanted a recommendation to mercy on the grounds that the accused pair had not *meant* to kill the girl. But, since neither men had admitted to the crime, one wonders how they knew?

A Woolwich case, in June 1920, a coal porter, when charged with murder of his wife he had said, 'I have had twenty years of it. Today, no dinner. She at a public house. ' I 'clumped her'. I was that mad I did not know what I did.' Perhaps a not an unreasonable defence – except that she had been strangled. However, since 'the injuries were inflicted in the course of a quarrel' he was found guilty of manslaughter and given 12 months imprisonment.[7] In Manchester in May, 1923, a man who had insured his wife's life then had gone around trying to hire someone to throw her off the balcony, got three years.[8]

Fortunately, someone in the judiciary had begun to notice this state of affairs. On 15 March, 1923, when trying a case of attempted murder by 26-year-old Bernard Anthony O'Sullivan who had become angry because a girl would not leave her fiancé for him and had struck her around the head with a flat iron eleven times, and had told a man who came along, 'If she does not die, I have disfigured her for life.' The jury had found him Not Guilty of Attempted Murder but Mr Justice Avory, gave him ten years for Wounding declaring that:

'crimes of violence, committed by men on woman, simply because the woman would not do exactly what the man desired, were much too prevalent in this country at the present time, and persons who committed such crimes were being encouraged in the

commission of them by the idea that even if they were convicted of murder, the extreme penalty of the law would not be carried out. [9]

A few days later a man, who had been acquitted by the jury of Attempted Murder for sending explosives by post, (with a gun primed to fire when the parcel was opened) to his ex-fiance and two of her relatives, because she had broken off with him. But Avory gave him seven years penal servitude for sending an Explosive Substance by Post with intent to do Grievous Bodily Harm and pointed out that this *another* instance of the kind of crime he had already denounced as being prevalent.[10]

Of course, Avory *was* known as 'the hanging judge', so some may have just seen this as disappointment. The suffragettes had noticed that the British legal system operated primarily in favour of men – natural when you have an entrenched patriarchy – human beings will always want things *their* way. The Women's Freedom League even had a regular item in their magazine satirically entitled *The Protected Sex* in which they recorded the comparable sentencing handed down to each sex and also noting that there were laws against women only, for example soliciting, which did not apply to men, and certainly did not for a very long time after the 1920s.[11]

As a policewoman in the 1950s it always struck me as rather droll that I would be going home after doing late duty at West End Central, which often included dealing with prostitutes arrested for this offence, and when I got off the bus in Bayswater Road and went to cross the road I would sometimes be solicited by men in cars. I would produce my warrant card, and snap, 'Read it. Now beat it!' And they did, to a crashing of gears, little knowing that they were *not* committing any offence and their wives were *not* about to find out. Men were 'protected'. A good proportion of the Golden Age writers were female and I am not sure whether they ever picked up on this sexual inequality in the law.

(However, as you doubtless know, women *were* free to be homosexual whilst for men it was still illegal.)

Meanwhile, Chief D I Mercer had been back on the South Coast, this time at Portsmouth in Hampshire. Clearly spreading his net wide to catch the murderers in the upmarket Eastbourne had done him no harm. This time, he was after the killer of Mary Pelham, alternately dubbed 'a flower seller' and 'a woman of 'the unfortunate class' – in other words a prostitute. She had been found with her head bashed in with a bottle and a scarf tied tightly around her neck after having been seen heading home with a sailor. That should be easy to solve, Mercer must have thought – a *sailor* in *Portsmouth*, our chief naval port.[12]

Soon, however, there was the familiar flurry of' possible suspects engendering excitement in the Press such as a mass identification parade of three thousand sailors at the Royal Naval Barracks – repeated four times in different clothing but alas not picked out by the female witnesses[13]. Then, another, smaller, parade at the Town Hall. The victim had boasted about her jewellery – might not robbery be a motive? And wasn't there smudges on some broken glass which could be fingerprints...?[14]

Then there was the 'Mysterious Horndean Visitor' who appeared to be a seafaring man but wore civilian clothes. He had said he was a deserter and displayed much agitation when reading of the murder in the *Evening News* (reported *The*

Portsmouth Evening News) and hadn't the victim told somebody she had a man at home waiting for her?

Matters reached a fever pitch when two Scotland Yard detectives waited at the dockside as the steamer *Babington* reached Dundee after a description of a suspect had been sent to ships which were equipped with wireless telegraphy.

But it was all in vain. Perhaps Press overkill this time. No-one was charged. The following March, 1924, news arrived of a seaman on board a British warship in the Mediterranean having confessed to the murder, becoming mentally deranged, then jumping into the sea and drowning. (After conferring, the Chief Constable and Scotland Yard announced that they attached no importance to this confession.)[15]

By then, Mercer was past caring anyway having retired due to 'an uncommon complaint' – pernicious anaemia – possibly not helped by his reported 'unflagging energy' which in some cases had led him to work for three days and two nights without resting.[16]

Despite his ex-colleagues answering *en masse* to the call for blood transfusions, Mercer died.

The Dundee Evening Telegraph gave him a long and fulsome obituary under the heading:

C.I.D. CHIEF WHO SPREAD NET FOR MURDERERS.
PRICE INSPECTOR PAID IN THE BOTTOMLEY HUNT
Man Who Had Nosed Into Every Vice-Hole in London

'Mercer of the Yard' was a born tracker of men, keen and relentless as a bloodhound on the trail, and well-fortified by his temperament against the tedium of a thousand pettifogging inquiries which are a part of every big case.[17] But they were sure

that it was the Bottomley hunt which had cost him his life.[18]

The man does appear to have been in the vanguard of the Yard's gradually improving attempts to connect with the public via The Press. Back in 1882 the new chief, Howard Vincent, had forbidden his officers to give *any* information to the gentlemen of the Press although, with experience, he didn't quite stick to this himself soon pointing out that the Press were a power which they must not omit to take into account. Indeed, they had just helped police catch the railway murderer Percy Mapleton by even having his picture published and certainly the Press turned out to be vital when it came to the capture of Crippen. But even Vincent received a reprimand from the Home Office for the extent in which he used Press adverts to hunt fugitives because, apparently, this was considered 'undignified'.

By the early Twenties, however, there had arrived a new means of asking the public for their help: BBC Radio. Initially, this conduit seems to have been used mainly for tracing missing persons but eventually, in 1933, it was to help catch a killer.

NOTES FOR CHAPTER 6

1. *Capital Crimes,* p188; *Golden Age of Murder, p388*
2. *Capital* Crimes, *p279. Wikipedia: Ethel Lina White, 'Early Years'*
3. *Ibid p279*
4. *Murder Guide to London,* p68
5. *The Woman Before Wallace, p144-5*
6. *Ibid, p274-285*
7. *The Times,* 21 February, 1921

8. *The Yorkshire Post,* 4 May, 1923
9. *The Times,* 5 May, 1923
10. *The Times,* 15 March, 1923
11. *The Times,* 16 March, 1923
12. *The British Policewoman: Her Story,* p16
13. *The Times, 29 January,* 1923
14. *Portsmouth Evening News,* 2 February, 1923
15. *Ibid,* 30 January, 1923
16.*Edinburgh Evening News,* 8 March, 1924
17. *The Times,* 22 March, 1924
18. *The Dundee Evening Telegraph,* 28 April, 1924. 'The Bottomley Hunt':* Complicated, very high profile case of Fraud against Horatio William Bottomley who got the public to invest in £1 Victory Bonds with which he financed his various schemes.

7

Déjà Vu

Issued by His Majestys' Stationary Office in 1925 was:

FINGER PRINT CLUES:
NOTES ON FINGER PRINT CLUES LEFT
BY CRIMINALS AT PLACES WHERE
A CRIME HAS BEEN COMMITTED.
BY
CHARLES S. COLLINS

Charles Stockley Collins headed Scotland Yard's Fingerprint Bureau and had given fingerprint evidence at the ground-breaking trial of the Stratton Brothers for the brutal murder of an elderly couple of shopkeepers back in 1905.

On the strength of one fingerprint, the pair were the first in the U.K. to be convicted of murder in which fingerprint evidence played a very important part, although the judge had warned the jury *not* to convict on that evidence *alone*. When the defence called the prints into question Collins fingerprinted one of the jury to demonstrate differences due to the pressure applied.[1]

A Dr J G Garson had appeared for the Stratton brothers

defence team but not only had he been discredited for his lack of up-to-date knowledge about fingerprints, but also for offering his 'expert' opinions to the prosecution as well, whilst heavily criticising police evidence on the subject.

The trial had opened on 5 May, 1905. The brothers were executed on 23 May and, on 20 July, *The Daily Express* took advantage of the enormous public interest in the new science by running a £100 prize detective story puzzle which the public were invited to solve. The plot centred on 'the mysterious death of a solicitor and the heroic efforts of his daughter to discover who did the deed. The clue is A FINGER PRINT on a tumbler and, in the course of the story, the fingerprints of all the characters are given, and by comparing them the problem can be solved.'

Unfortunately, their fingerprint crash course (advertised ahead of time) came from the pen of the 'celebrated expert finger-print witness', Dr J G Garson.

Possibly, when commissioning him, *The Daily Express* had heeded the cries from *The Lancet* and other sources which deplored the fact that fingerprinting evidence was being left in the hands of clodhopping policemen rather than medical men whose evidence would not only be more scientifically accurate but above suspicion.

This claim was countered in a letter to the Editor from the Chief Constable of Staffordshire who was of the opinion that nine out of ten doctors made the *worst witnesses in the world*. *The Daily Express* did save face however by stating that, given their experience in solving crimes, policemen *would* stand a chance of winning the prize.

The Henry Fingerprint classification system[2] the Yard

was using had already received worldwide attention the previous year when one of the six police officers, sent to St Louis World Fair to guard the Queen's Jubilee presents which were on exhibition, included Detective Sergeant Ferrier of the Met's Fingerprint Branch. Whilst there, he gave a fingerprint demonstration to the International Association of Police Chiefs and was overwhelmed by enquiries from them.

There is little doubt that this demo helped sound the death knell of the French Anthropometric or Bertillonage identification system, (which relied largely on taking measurements of limbs, fingers, ears and so on) and caused a worldwide swing to the Henry fingerprinting classification system by most of the English-speaking world and elevated the reputation of Scotland Yard.

The Metropolitan Police (desperately looking for a reliable identification system) along with many other countries *had* adopted Bertillonage but not only found it labour intensive but that it relied heavily on the accuracy of those taking the measurements. Fingerprinting was simpler, quicker and utterly individual and undeniable – once you had an accurate classification system. Bertillonage *had*, however, encouraged the Metropolitan Police to take side as well as front-facing views of the suspects which gave a better impression of the person, and also to photograph hands, which could be indicative of their work and lifestyle, and reveal helpful scars.

Stockley Collins's booklet was obviously meant primarily to assist other British police forces most of whom had been relying on sending their crime scene prints to the Yard to be checked but were now setting up their own systems. Fingerprint patterns and ridge characteristics were shown and the best methods of locating them on the glass, knives and so forth illustrated; how to reveal them with powders etc then to record them using a camera with a bellows extension twice the focal length of the lens used. Also, how to preserve and pack those objects being sent to the Yard. Collins had already produced a pamphlet giving telegraphic codes for fingerprints and the Branch was now receiving messages using these codes from as far away as Australia and New Zealand.

Meanwhile, members of the fingerprint branch were constantly called upon countrywide to talk juries through fingerprint evidence whilst showing them photographic enlargements because, almost twenty years after the Stratton case, fingerprint identification was still not automatically accepted. Juries had to be convinced and the Yard's fingerprint men had become experts at doing this.

On Thursday, 1 May, 1924, ex-Divisional Inspector Beard contacted Chief Constable Wensley and told him 'a rather singular story'.

A woman of his acquaintance had found a Waterloo Station cloakroom ticket which had dropped from one of her husband's pockets and, a little suspicious about his recent absences, she had asked Beard to find out what the ticket was for? So far, Beard had gone to Waterloo station where he had discovered that it was a ticket for a locked Gladstone bag and by lifting up the flaps he had managed to get a glimpse inside and had seen some women's clothing which appeared to be bloodstained.

Wensley realised that there could be an innocent explanation for all this. Maybe they were the belongings of a woman with whom the husband was associating? Nonetheless, he asked Chief Inspector Percy Savage, a man of 24 years police experience and whose father had been a policeman, to take a look into the matter.[3] Savage had his officers keep watch on the cloak-room telling them that, if someone tried to claim the bag, to bring them in and inform him or Wensley.

The following evening they had the husband. He turned out to be Patrick Mahon, a good-looking, well-spoken young man with an engaging manner. It transpired that, due to his wife's influence, he had recently become a sales manager in the firm where she was a secretary. The bag was opened to reveal a torn pair of bloomers, two pieces of new, white silk, stained with blood and grease, a blue silk scarf, a large cook's knife and a tennis bag bearing the initials E.B.K.

Initially, Mahon told them that the bag had been used to carry meat home for his dogs. Savage pointed out that you don't usually wrap dog's meat in silk and that he was not satisfied with his explanation. There followed a protracted silence before Mahon decided he would tell them 'the truth'.

During an interview which lasted from 11pm until two the following morning Mahon described his ten-month affair with secretary, Miss Emily Kaye. She had begun pressing him to elope and, to satisfy her, he had agreed to 'a love experiment' which involved a holiday in a bungalow in that spot now familiar to Scotland Yard – The Crumbles in Eastbourne. Whilst there, Mahon told them, he and Emily had quarrelled and she had thrown a coal axe at him. It had struck him a glancing blow. He saw red and they struggled. 'She was a very big, strong girl.' Then Emily had fallen and struck her head on an iron coal scuttle. He had been unable to revive her and realised that she was dead.

The following day he had returned to London where he purchased a knife and a saw with which to dismember her body. He boiled some portions of the flesh, packed them in the bag and threw them from railway carriage windows between Waterloo and Richmond on his return home.

Bizarrely, back in London he had made contact with another young woman whom he invited to stay with him at the Pevensey Bay bungalow on the coming Good Friday. He would, he explained to Savage, have gone stark raving mad had he been there alone. The young woman had stayed for the weekend whilst Miss Kaye's headless body was there in a locked trunk which, Mahon told her, contained books.

So, it was back to The Crumbles for the Yard men where they were joined by the pathologist, Sir Bernard Spilsbury. He agreed that the coal scuttle appeared too flimsy to account for a serious injury and suggested that she had been killed by a blow to the head. Since the head was missing – Mahon told them he had burned it on the fire – this could scarcely be proved.

Back in London detectives were now learning more about Mahon who, it turned out, was a compulsive womaniser constantly picking up women; had a criminal record, and was clearly rather strange. He had served twelve months for embezzlement and five years for breaking into a bank, stunning a woman with a hammer and, as she recovered consciousness, kissing and fondling her and asking for forgiveness. Also, that Emily had taken her savings with her to The Crumbles because she imagined that they were going to be married and go to live in South Africa, and Mahon had already spent some of these savings.

The stench in the bungalow proved too much, even for the

experienced Spilsbury, so he took his work out onto a bench in the garden. Amongst other things he discovered was that the victim was six months pregnant and, whilst they were working, that Savage was handling pieces of putrid flesh and placing them in a bucket. Pointing out the dangers of infection he asked, 'Are there no rubber gloves?' There were not, and never had been.

Consequently, Spilsbury and members of the team set out to plan a bag which would hold everything they thought that a member of the Murder Squad would need when answering a call for assistance, from specimen jars to screwdrivers plus rubber gloves, and which was to become famous as The Murder Bag.[4]

When it came to his summing up to the jury at the end of Mahon's trial Mr Justice Avory came on with all guns blazing:

'Counsel for the prisoner', he said, *'told you yesterday it was open to you to find the prisoner guilty either of murder or manslaughter or to find him not find him not guilty of any offence. I would have been glad if learned counsel had explained to you upon what principle of law he invited you to say that the prisoner in this case might be not guilty at all. In my view, the only ground upon which he could be found not guilty of any offence would be that in taking away the life of the deceased woman he was acting in self-defence, which means it was necessary for him to kill her in order to save his own life, or to save himself from such serious bodily harm that his life would have been endangered.*

It will be for you to say upon the facts of the case whether there is any possible ground upon which you could come to the conclusion that it was necessary for him to kill this woman in order to save his own life.'

Avory went on to point up the damning prosecution evidence – a great deal had been said about the dead woman being tall, strong and athletic – well, they had seen *him* and she was a woman of 5ft 7in in height. Then again, at 3.40 pm on the Tuesday afternoon, he had sent a message to the other young woman, Miss Duncan, asking her to meet him on the Wednesday to arrange for her to come down Eastbourne on the Friday. How did he know *then* that he and Miss Kaye were going to have that falling out on the Tuesday evening which would make him free to carry out this fresh intrigue on the Wednesday?

Why had he gone to the trouble of destroying Miss Kaye's skull so utterly and scattering the remnants in the sand if it hadn't been to hide her injuries? And *why* hadn't he asked for help for her that Tuesday evening – there was a telephone in the house and a neighbour next door. And *why*, and this was the killer, had he bought the large knife and saw in Victoria Street *before* the time he went down to The Crumbles that *first* time – *with* Miss Kaye – not *after* she was dead? They were told it was to cut up the meat they were going to eat when there already was an efficient carving knife at the bungalow.

And there was more. But it was enough.

He was found guilty and sentenced to death.[5]

According to Wensley, the case which rounded off 1924 was a copycat of the Mahon murder although he did not use that term but rather 'The tendency to imitate in methods of murder'[6] although one wonders why anyone would want to imitate a crime which had ended as disastrously as the Mahon case.

This new story began on Friday, 5 December, 1924, when

23-year-old Elsie Cameron left home with a suitcase telling no-one of her destination but leaving a note saying she was going away for the weekend and should be back on Monday. It was presumed she was going to see her fiancé, the 24-year-old Norman Thorne, an unsuccessful chicken farmer who lived in Crowborough, not far north of Eastbourne. Elsie did not return on Monday but a letter addressed to her from Thorne did. It asked why had she not arrived on the Friday?

Elsie failed to surface and became the **Missing London Typist**[7]. On 12 January, 1925, 31 days after she went missing, Scotland Yard was asked for their assistance and Detective Chief Inspector John Gillan, ' a strong and astute officer'[8] arrived in Crowborough and began interrogating Thorne.

A local farm labourer thought he had seen a woman resembling Miss Cameron's photograph in Crowborough on 5 December. Thorne admitted that he *had expected* her on that day and had gone to the railway station to meet her but that she had not arrived. Nine police constables, drawn from the neighbourhood villages, began digging on Thorne's Farm, supervised by DCI Gillan. Three hours later they found Elsie's suitcase buried two foot down near the farm gate. Further interviews with Thorne persuaded him, as with Mahon, that *now* was the time to tell 'the truth'.

His story led more police to hurry to the farm by motor car and bicycle late that night to dig again, this time by moonlight and with 'electric torches' until, in a chicken run, they found Elsie's dismembered body.[9]

Thorne's 'truth' was that he had fallen for another girl and tried to break off his relationship with Elsie but she would have none of it and was determined he should marry her because she was pregnant (as it turned out, Emily Kaye *had* been but Elsie was *not*). He admitted that she *had* arrived on 5 December but that evening he had had to leave her to meet the other girl and, when he came home he found her hanging from a beam in the hut. Terrified about the likely consequences he cut up the body and burned her clothes.

However, there were no marks on the soft wood of the beam to indicate a hanging having taken place. Gillan and his sergeant experimented with appropriate weights which indicated, that if Thorne was really telling the truth, there *should* have been. And there were bruises on her body which, according to the prosecution's pathologist, Spilsbury again, indicated a struggle and an assault. He found *no* evidence that she had actually died from hanging. Other expert medical witnesses disagreed but the jury chose to believe Spilsbury. Thorne was found Guilty and sentenced to death.

The case became famous as evidence of Spilsbury's now papal infallibility. Indeed Thorne, in a letter to his father on the eve of his execution, is reported to have claimed that he was a martyr to Spilsburyism.[10] However, the pathologist's biographers (Douglas G Browne & E V Tullett) build up a convincing case against the evidence of the *other* (numerous) 'experts'[11].

'It was a point of significance, too,' wrote Wensley, 'although I do not think it was brought out at the trial, that among things found in the hut (in which Thorne lived) were a number of newspaper cuttings on the Mahon case, and several books on pathology.'[12]

An Appeal, which Thorne expected to succeed, failed and he was taken from the court crying, 'It isn't fair! I didn't do it!'[13]

*   *   *

Of course, murder cases were by no means the chief occupation of the Metropolitan Police detectives at this time. The rise of the motor car may have led to motor bandits but it also spelled the beginning of the end of some traditional offences such as horse chanting and van dragging.

Horse chanters had bought decrepit and worn out horses, doped them and sold them on as sound of wind and limb. For many, this had been flourishing and lucrative work which had also kept the detectives busy. Van draggers would capture vans loaded with merchandise then release the horse and let it wander off because owners could easily identify it.

While such offences were dying out others, such as rogue fortune-telling and spiritualism, fraudulent marriage bureaux and bigamy had all become more prevalent. People were increasingly eager to get in touch with those they had lost in the war and the surplus women wanted husbands.

DI Ferrier, who related several sad tales about the latter in his book *Crooks and Crime,* claimed it was usually women who were duped by the marriage bureau and bigamists and, whilst he seemed to overlook their more vulnerable situation he *did* admit that widowers were also often pathetically eager to remarry. But, of course, there *were* fewer widowers than widows and men were now at a premium given the numbers lost in the war.

Other traditional crimes such as burglary, shoplifting, fraud and confidence trickery still flourished and quite often it was a case of working out *who* of those known to the detectives was likely to have committed this particular sort of crime and going after them. If the ground below the window through which the burglar had gained access had been wired (with thin wire, held by wooden stakes to trip up pursuers), that would be *Quiet Joe* who always worked alone. If the victims were working class, their houses backed onto fields and they were robbed on a Friday night that might well be *Flannel Foot* (AKA *Gimlet Jim* and *Footpad Jack*) who was after their weekly pay-packet.

Whilst not providing the venues for the sensational murder cases depicted in some detective fiction, the great country houses were, in 1922-23, being ransacked by a couple of rogues responsible for some sensational art thefts. They were picky thieves too. Perhaps a couple of Gainsboroughs, a few choice miniatures, and odds and ends of the better jewellery. And they left no fingerprints. They travelled about the country by train, hiring bicycles to get from the stations to the next estate. Press coverage was fulsome in praise of their good taste and delighted in the story of one unaware country policeman helping them mend a puncture.

'I do not know how many police forces were concerned in one way or another' wrote Wensley 'but this was a striking example of a case where a national detective service, which could have dealt with the investigation as a whole, would have been of effective use.'[14]

The guilty pair (George Smithson, aged 31, and George Ingram, aged 30) were caught at last by the Scottish Police when returning to the railway station carrying valuables from their latest hoist. One was sentenced to 6 years, the other, who had committed fewer crimes, to four.

Then they volunteered to come to England to have the rest of their depredations taken into consideration so that, on release, they would not have any remaining jobs hanging over their heads.[15]

The pair were brought to London by DI Goodwillie to whom they admitted breaking into thirty-six English and Welsh houses – as far as they could remember. Their list of victims read like a page from *Burke's Landed Gentry*. To Wensley, they appeared rather proud of themselves relating their exploits 'as if they merited praise'.[16]

They were given eight and six years to run concurrently with their Scottish sentences. They were careful not to betray their receivers but, as many of these were already in the Yard's hands a great deal of the property was recovered.

NOTES FOR CHAPTER SEVEN

1. Cherrill of the Yard, p35

2. Named after the Metropolitan Police Commissioner Sir Edward Henry who devised the classification system

3. Detective Days, p273-275

4. Murder Squad, p66

5. The Times, 21 July, 1924

6. Detective Days, p276

7. The Times 13 January, 1925

8. Detective Days, p277

9. The Times, 16 January, 1925

10. Carol Westron, Mystery Women, 6 July,2016

11. Bernard Spilsbury: His Life and Cases, p105-201

12. Detective Days, p279

13. Murders of the Black Museum, p298

14. Detective Days p181

15. Banbury Advertiser, 5 July, 1923 and *Sunday Post*, 29 July

1923
16. Detective Days, p182

8
Local Feeling

Despite some claims that few Golden Age murders actually took place in great country houses, Anthony Berkeley Cox, the next Golden Ager to enter the field in 1925, set his first detective novel in such a place. His sleuth, in *The Layton Court Mystery,* was another in the classic gentleman amateur detective mode – with a difference – no charm. Roger Sheringham was rude and offensive, based, Berkeley claimed, 'on an offensive person I once knew.' At the time he imagined it would be amusing to have an offensive detective.'[1]

Cox himself was upper class and had been educated at Sherborn Public School and University College, London, before joining the army in the Great War. Now a journalist, he was to become a leading light in the Golden Age genre but this first attempt was published anonymously in the familiar just-to-see-if-I-can-do-it, fashion.

Roger Sheringham, was a house guest at Layton Court when his jolly, middle-aged host, Mr Victor Stanworth, was found shot dead in the library. The author lets his readers in on all the evidence as his deliberately fallible detective stumbles along building up his case.

On recent republishing this book received mixed Amazon reviews from 'wonderful lively book. First rate dialogue' to 'stumbles a little too much' and 'Definitely not "Golden Age".

Two more new detective novelists emerged that year: Major John Charles Street (who was to write as John Rhode and under several other names) and Ronald Arbuthnott Knox. Rhodes's first detective novel was *The Paddington Mystery* and his leading character an independent researcher, Dr Lancelot Priestly, who delighted in scientific controversy and provided technical assistance to his friend, Chief Inspector Hanslet. *The Paddington Mystery* received a rather lukewarm welcome from *The Scotsman:* 'if conventional, is readable and pleasantly baffling'. Later, crime fiction novelist and critic Julian Symons, found John Rhode to be one of the 'humdrums'[2] as did H.R.F. Keating citing all the characteristics of the middle-ranking books of the period, 'ingenuity of plot, cardboardity of character, chunter of story'.[3]

More lively than the humdrums, Symons thought, were the Farceurs – such as Ronald Arbuthnott Knox, who never allowed the faintest breath of seriousness to disturb the desperate facetiousness of his style[4]. Given that author's day job, this was surprising.

Eton and Balliol educated Knox had become an Anglican priest in 1912 then, in 1918, was ordained a Catholic then, the following year, became a Roman Catholic Priest. *The Viaduct Murder,* his first fictional effort as Ronald Knox, features another amateur detective who gets everything wrong. (Knox believed in fairness to the reader and later published his own set of rules for the genre.) When advertising his book in *The Times* Methuen quoted the *Daily Mail*'s opinion of *Father*

Ronald Knox's book as 'A brilliant detective story . . . by an author whose wit and style have already won him a wide public. His pages are strewn with good things.'

In January, 1926, Knox did something quite daring, and perhaps rather odd particularly given his calling. In one of his regular BBC radio programmes Knox broadcast a simulated live report of a supposed revolution which was sweeping London: *Broadcasting from the Barricades.* In this, were live reports of people being lynched, and supposed band music from the Savoy Hotel mixed with purported destruction of the hotel by trench mortars, and the Houses of Parliament being flattened. It was Broadcast on a snowy weekend when much of the UK was unable to get newspapers so there was a minor panic. It was thought that the broadcast may have been the inspiration for Orson Wells's *War of the Worlds* broadcast which caused such a panic in 1938 and Wells actually admitted this in an interview with Peter Bogdanovich in 1992.[5]

The first two events that really gripped the public's attention in the year of 1926 was, of course, the General Strike in May which began when coal miners refused to give way to the mine owners who wanted them to work longer hours for less pay. Sympathetic workers in transport, the print, gas, electricity and others had joined them. The resulting chaos encouraged many of the public to act as volunteers – including wealthy young men who had such fun driving the buses. The TUC backed down, the strike failed and the men had little choice but to go back to work for the 13% less pay and the hour a day longer.

The other event was the disappearance of the now well-known authoress Agatha Christie in the December of that year. No-one knew where she had gone nor why. Her financial prospects certainly looked good having just had published her ground-breaking novel, *The Murder of Roger Ackroyd,* to great acclaim. She had always known comfort and financial security having been born into a wealthy upper-middle class family living in an attractive country house in spacious grounds where she enjoyed an indulged childhood.

There *had* been a blip when Daddy, who normally spent his days at his club, failed to keep an eye on the funds. But that did ensure some long holidays abroad in sunny climes whilst they rented out said handsome house. Nonetheless, Agatha seemed to dislike anyone getting the idea that they may have been wealthy. She dismissed the idea in her autobiography making the point that everyone had servants and the really rich had more than them and also had motor cars.[6]

The hunt to find the missing writer involved over a thousand police officers plus members of the public. Sir Arthur Conan Doyle and Dorothy L Sayers were consulted to no effect. She was eventually recognised in a Harrogate Hotel and went home. No explanation was offered but it seems a wayward husband may have been the reason.

Most of Scotland Yard's detectives came from working class backgrounds and had only very basic education. No public schools nor universities. In Victorian times, when some of the current leaders had joined, their lessons on how to become police officers had also been extremely basic. They were merely given drill, spent some time listening to cases at court and were issued with an instruction book on the various laws and police duties before being taken learning beats by older constables and from them picked up their good or bad habits. Extraordinary really, particularly since many of them were from rural backgrounds and had had little exposure to big city life.

At last, in 1907, a Met Police Training School was opened and recruits were given eight weeks tuition in police duty, general education, physical training, self defence and first aid although drill still loomed large. There was no training on how to be a detective.

The first real-life London murder of 1926 was discovered in an ordinary Camden Town house on the morning of New Year's Day. The body of the victim, 16-year-old Polly Walker (immediately dubbed a 'girl cashier' by *The Times*), was found in her bedroom with a silk stocking tied tightly around her neck and six wounds to her head which had been inflicted by a poker and a pair of tongs. It was the silk stocking which had killed her by strangulation.

Detective Inspector Hambrook was called to the scene. In 1920 he had been put in charge of the Flying Squad but later that same year had become a Divisional DI in charge of 32 detectives covering S Division which stretched from Marylebone to the Northern edges of the Met. (Perhaps his Gung Ho attitude had caused Wensley to move him on?)

He found Polly's bedroom in a state of great disorder but soon realised that this was *not* going to be a difficult case to crack. Mrs Kathleen Lukey, who lived in the room below, recalled hearing a scream around 9a.m. Shortly afterwards there was the sound of hurried footsteps down the stairs. She recognised these instantly due to the simple fact that they belonged to a regular visitor to the house, Eugene De Vere, who had only one leg.

Deformities of any kind are a boon to a detective when it comes to identification and, in the days before health and safety at work and the lack of much corrective surgery, there tended to be more of these then – which helped compensate for the lack of much forensic aid.

De Vere's leg had been amputated due to a childhood deformity and he wore an artificial leg on which he stumped along. He struggled to earn a living. For a while playing an accordion to entertain theatre queues, but he had no regular employment and Polly's widowed mother had taken pity on him and invited him in for meals.

'He was down and out,' said her son Frank, 'and he had no friends in the world. We were sorry for him and thought we were doing a Christian act in helping him. We treated him like a brother.'

Unfortunately, de Vere fell heavily for Frank's sister Polly, a rather frail girl who soon found his attentions overwhelming. Just before Christmas 1925 the family decided that they should stop his visits but postponed telling him until after the festivities. During their Christmas and New Year parties he became aggressively jealous of an old family friend, a young chauffeur named Miall.

The next lunchtime, when Mrs Walker returned from her work as a cleaner at a 'picture palace', she found Polly's body. Not only had De Vere taken her daughter's life but he had also stolen a gold pocket watch and several other valuable items belonging to the son Frank. He pawned them at various places on his way out of London sending the tickets to Mrs Walker.

Messages went out to police and pawn shops on de Vere's route and, within 48 hours, he was recognised by a Hertfordshire policeman whom he told he had walked most of the thirty-two miles from London. Meanwhile, police had been making some enquiries and discovered that De Vere was Scottish and that his real name was Ewen Anderson Stitchwell.

Stitchwell claimed that Polly had asked what he wanted that morning, called him a beast and bit his finger. 'He picked up the tongs, ran after her,' Hambroook recalled, 'and hit her on the head. He believed he picked up a poker as well, but he did not know what he was doing. "She fell on the floor," de Vere continued. I picked her up and put her on the bed. I picked up the stocking and tied it around her neck.' His defence counsel declared that due to the 'provocation' a verdict of manslaughter ought to be brought in. Maybe the judges had had their fingers rapped about letting young men get away with murder for Mr Justice Salter did not agree, pointing out that, to justify a verdict of manslaughter the provocation had to be intolerable to the average man – more than human flesh and blood could bear'. Nonetheless, when the jury found him guilty of wilful murder they recommended mercy due to 'strong provocation and the peculiar mentality of the prisoner' but his appeal failed and he was hanged.[7]

Things had moved on a little for the Flying Squad. They still operated from two large vans – one for the south and one for the north side of the river. Their mobility had been proving effective but a communication problem remained. To contact the Yard, they had to pull up beside a public telephone so that one of the crew could ring in. Experiments with Morse code proved successful so, in September, 1923, transmitting and receiving apparatus was installed in the vans, as were trained operators.

There remained problems with blind spots and the large aerials erected on the van roofs not only gained the vans the title 'the bedsteads' but also alerted criminals to their presence and identity.

Fortunately, the success of the squad also began to have a marked effect when judges began handing out stiffer sentences to the criminal gangs.

Meanwhile, in Stoke-on-Trent, Staffordshire, on the evening of 23 October, 1925, the wife of 62-year-old warehouseman, John Porter, waited for her husband to come home from work at the Alexander Potteries although when he failed to arrive she didn't worry, just assumed that he was going to work all night, as he sometimes did. In the morning she sent their daughter in with toast and tea for his breakfast. Alas, the door of the fitting room, where John worked, was locked. Padlocked in fact, and there was no sign of him elsewhere. Eventually, the door was unlocked and her father's body was found lying on the floor in a pool of blood, with dreadful head injuries.

John Porter was reputedly a mild-mannered man so nobody could understand who and why anyone should have done this to him. The only hint of anything suspicious was that he had collected his wages that day but now only about 10 shillings were found on him. It was a mystery that the local police were finding extremely hard to solve.

Indeed, by 5th November, nearly two weeks later, *The Lancashire Evening Post,* was commenting that, 'although the police have ceaselessly followed up clues in various directions their investigations have led them very little nearer to the discovery of the murderer.' Also that, 'They have not yet decided to call in the assistance of Scotland Yard.'

It was to be another couple *of* weeks before *The Liverpool Echo* was to announce what they called 'a sequel' to the murder of an elderly man who, it would be recalled had been found dead three weeks before 'his head being smashed' and that, following an appeal by Porter's son, the arrival of Detective Chief Inspector Gillan and Detective Sergeant Hastings from Scotland Yard 'at the request of Stoke on Trent Police'.[8] So, not exactly a pristine crime scene nor a fresh investigation to welcome them?

Soon, the *Echo was* reporting a *result*: the arrest by the Yard's Detective Chief Inspector Gillan, of 24-year-old boiler-firer Henry Adams for the murder of John Porter. When charged, Adams had said, 'Yes. I don't wish to say anything beyond what I have already told Mr Gillan.'[9]

What Adams had told 'Mr Gillan' and what the Stipendiary court was informed about the following day, was that on that fateful evening he had gone to the fitting shop to fill his lamp and taken a torchlight with him. "I was just on the point of opening the tap of the oil barrel when Porter entered and picked up the lamp hammer which was on top of the bench, and walked down the shop towards me. He said, 'Hallo you ------- thing, you have brought that stinking thing down again (meaning the torchlight)'. I said, "What is the matter with you. You don't have to pay for it." He then struck at me and caught me over my right eye with his fist. I then slipped to the floor on my right hand, and my fist came into contact with the hoop of iron round the barrel. Looking up, I saw Porter was threatening me with a hammer. I jumped up and took it away from him.

From then, until the end, I have no clear recollection of what occurred but I must have hit him on the head with the hammer. He never spoke after I had hit him.'

Someone certainly *had* hit Porter on the head. There were eight wounds, five of them causing skull fractures and one resulting in 'a hole right through to the brain'.

Adams rounded off his statement to Gillan by saying, 'I had not the slightest intention of killing Jack Porter. I bore him no malice even though he was frequently on at me.'

Suspicions had clearly already led the local police towards Adams due to his being reported absent at certain periods that night by a couple of fellow workers.

The next day, Mr John Newman, the Engineer in charge, told the court that Porter had been an easy-tempered man not given to using foul and abusive language (such as Adams had claimed) and that Adams, when he saw him, had had a small mark under his right eye which looked like a bruise dying away.

Workman, James Ibbs, had not been able to find Adams to tell him he was leaving so the engines could be stopped at 8pm, so he just left. Charles Edward Wilshaw, 'an odd man on ovens' couldn't find Adams until ten to two in the morning and then saw scratches his face. Biscuit placer, William Ward, had seen him going through the saggar-house towards the fitting shop at ten or twenty minutes past seven.

Local Detective Inspector McEvoy said he had asked Adams for the clothes he had worn that evening and had them examined but no bloodstains were found. Gillan praised the efforts of the local police and they appeared to have co-operated with him without any difficulty. They had clearly worked hard taking at least 72 statements from the workers including several from Adams. They shared all of this with Gillan who, having also interviewed Adams several times, now asked him if he would like to speak to him alone and he said yes so D I McEvoy and his sergeant left. Then Adams made his confession to DCI Gillan, first of all, telling him he had told lies to McEvoy.

On 10 December the cover of POLICE NEWS was devoted to a picture story of the DRAMATIC ARREST IN THE POTTERIES MURDER CASE with illustrations showing John Porter and Henry Adams, who according to them was a well-built young man with a caste in his left eye. There were scenes of '*Where the Body Was Found, Adams being charged, Adams walking to the police court and the Thousands of people waiting outside in vain for the arrival of the prisoner* (because they had changed the venue – twice).

By the third day of the Committal hearings, Adams had acquired a defence solicitor, Mr Collis, and his client, Adams, was now totally innocent. His confession, which he had made because he was scared and confused, became 'the alleged statement', and Collis began throwing every accusation he could think of at Chief Inspector Gillan.

According to him, Gillan had come up to the Potteries having read all the statements and formed in his own mind the theory of how the crime had been committed. This was his last chance of getting home on this case so he had exercised the methods known as the Third Degree on Adams. He had told him he was 'in the sludge' and 'had guilt written all over him' and that if he took his advice the only charge would be of manslaughter due to self defence. If not, he would throw him to the local police the result of which would be The Gallows. Gillan had claimed he had no axe to grind and no promotion to seek because he was at the top of the tree.

Gillan fought back responding 'Ridiculous!' to some of the most outrageous suggestions and even claimed that obviously some of the witnesses 'had been got at' but, of course, the Press lapped all this up and more and more of them gave it prominent coverage – often edited and garbled.

The accused obliged by going into the witness box and claiming he had been scared and confused. The local police resisted efforts to blacken Gillan by having words put into their mouths by Collis and being asked some equally melodramatic questions such whether they thought the work-room hammer 'was screaming for justice'.

However, the most vital evidence came from Sergeant Rushton, of Longton, one of the six highly industrialised towns which made up the city of Stoke (Fenton, Hanley,Tunstall, Burslam, Longton, Stoke). Having escorted Adams to Strangeways Gaol, he now gave evidence that the prisoner had seemed deep in thought and then said, 'They can't get me for murder only manslaughter, because of self defence' and went on 'Porter was very nasty that morning. He picked up a hammer and attempted to strike me. I took it off him. When I got the hammer I lost control of myself, and I do not know what happened afterwards. I have told Mr Gillan what I have told you.' From someone with no axe to grind this fully supported Gillan's evidence but was reported as 'another alleged statement'.

Also, the night watchman Green, who was recalled at his own request to insist that it was the *prisoner* and *not* the *deceased* to whom he referred in his evidence as being of a peculiar temperament and to be moody but also that he had never heard either the accused or the deceased use filthy or abusive language.

But there was no stopping it now: 'ALLEGED BULLYING BY THE POLICE' trumpeted *The Scotsman* going on to describe *how* the workmen witnesses had been treated. The watchman claimed that Gillan had seemed vexed with him because he wouldn't describe the mark on Adams face as a finger-mark and had told him that they had no sense of their duties as citizens. Another employee complained that the Yard men had taken him to a public house and given him half a pint of beer. 'They kept on pumping me and asking if I knew Harry Adams and what sort of fellow he was.'

Which you would think a reasonable question, particularly from a police officer in a strange environment, amongst a populace quite new to him and dealing with a case grown icy cold before they had even got there. Both these workman witnesses had words almost put into their mouth by Collis: 'Did he suggest that you were screening Adams or connected with the crime yourself?' Eliciting the reply that Gillan had been vexed with him and when he couldn't come up with further information. Tucker then suggested:

'May I put it shortly that he bullied you into saying something you would not say?'

' Yes, sir' was the inevitable reply.

Come the trial there was more – such as this, from the *Newcastle Evening Chronicle*:

METHODS OF THE YARD
Grave Allegations in Murder Trial
Police Pilloried by Witnesses
However, when it came to the verdict the most pertinent

point was put by the prosecuting counsel, Sir Reginald Coventry, 'whatever the jury thought of the confession that Adams was alleged to have made to Chief Inspector Gillan they must find an answer to the statement he made twenty four hours later (to the police escort), when he said that after he saw Porter with the hammer he did not know what happened.'

And the judge wasn't having any nonsense either telling the jury that in his opinion Gillan's statement had *not* been obtained by threats or promises and that it seemed to him incredible that an officer of Gillan's great experience and high position would be guilty of any such absurd, nonsensical conduct claimed by the defence, but they had to make up their own minds.

Which they did, very quickly in twenty-five minutes returning a verdict of guilty of Manslaughter, after which, Adams was given 7 years penal servitude.

It was revealed that he had a record of several minor offences and had served three years in a Borstal for breaking into a factory but he had not previously been convicted of violence.[10] But it was not to end there. Adams appealed and permission to do so was granted due to the questions about that statement and he was granted legal aid. But the Appeal failed. The judges found there was no threat nor inducement.

Certainly there were errors on all sides – what was Gillan doing interviewing Adams alone? What was the local D I McEvoy doing allowing it but he was probably relieved and why did he ask Adams for the work clothes and boots he wore *that night* and not *all* his work clothes? And Defence Solicitor Collis over-doing the accusatory melodramatic language so that Gillan could justifiably answer 'Ridiculous!' and claim some witnesses had been 'got at' which they clearly had and so that even the judges could point out how overblown it all was.

And, of course, probably what all this was about: admit your guilt but make it appear more forgiveable – and receive a Manslaughter verdict --- or challenge it and risk ending up at the gallows which was what Gillan – with his memory of Thorne sobbing when realising he was to die – may have been recommending.

NOTES FOR CHAPTER 8

1. *Golden Age of Murder*, p42
2. *Bloody Murder*, p114-115
3. *Whodunnit*, p223
4. *Bloody Murder*, p115
5. *Wikipedia: Ronald Knox. Ref Wells*
6. *Agatha Christie: An Autobiography*, p28-9, p180-181
7. *Hambrook of the Yard*, p166-171; *The Times* 9 January, 1926, and 12 January, 1926
8. *Liverpool Echo*, 19 November 1925
9. *Ibid, 2 December*, 1925
10. *The Scotsman*,1 March, 1926

9

Deja Vu Again

Detective novels of the Golden Age may have failed to mention the 1926 General Strike but two of their writers, the left-wing couple Margaret and Douglas Cole, became active supporting the workers involved. Later, they became disillusioned believing that the Strike – which actually left the miners no better off – had been deliberately provoked by the Government. But, as Martin Edwards points out in *The Golden Age of Murder*, 'The Coles kept in touch with the working classes by engaging three servants. The children were looked after by a nurse, and an unemployed Yorkshire miner and his wife were hired to do the housework.'

As for the continuing real crime scene there was a definite sense of having been there before about the developments on 10 May in the following year of 1927. The fact that it was a warm day was not appreciated in the Charing Cross Railway Station Left Luggage office which was pervaded by a nasty smell. This was traced to an unusual large, black, wickerwork trunk with a letter A painted on each end and I.F.A. on the lid, which had been brought in several days earlier. An attached label was addressed to F Austin, St Leonards.

A police constable was called, the trunk opened and found, beneath some brown paper, was the body of a woman. Her arms and legs had been removed and each limb separately wrapped and neatly tied with string. A duster was wrapped around her head.

What was quickly to be dubbed *THE CHARING CROSS TRUNK MURDER* was handed over to the Yard's Chief Detective Inspector George Cornish, the ex-farmer from Wiltshire, who, as a Divisional Detective Inspector, had arrested young Jacoby back in 1922.

The Mr F. Austin on the label was soon counted out of the running as a suspect but a name 'P Holt' and some laundry marks on blood-stained garments in the trunk quickly proved fruitful. In fact, within twenty-four hours, they had traced the Holt family who lived in Chelsea. It transpired that one of the garments belonged to the daughter of the house but she was alive and well. However, her mother *was* able to identify the body as that of a 'Mrs Roles' who, the previous year, had been temporarily employed by them as a cook.

By the next morning Cornish had found *Mr* Roles but it soon became clear that he had been no longer involved with the victim and was not a suspect. Also, that her real name had been Mrs Bonati. *Mr* Bonati proved to be an Italian waiter but he had been separated from his wife for some time and so *he* was not a suspect either but, Wensley noted, that they had 'gleaned a number of facts about her habits and temperament that might prove useful'[1]. Irritatingly, he does not reveal what these were. However, she proved to have a number of man friends – but all had alibis.

Meanwhile, there was the unusual trunk to trace.

Fortunately, a dealer in second-hand baggage in Brixton Road recognised a newspaper picture of the trunk as having been purchased from him by a man who told him he required a cheap old thing to hold some clothes and oddments for shipping abroad. Unfortunately, the dealer was hazy about the man's appearance and the date of purchase.

Various other possible leads led nowhere and the investigation began to slow down. The left-luggage attendants could not remember *when* the trunk was deposited or by *whom* – so *many* travellers came and went . . . Of course, the murder was receiving a great deal of coverage in the Press so that another potential witness's memory was jogged when a young boot-black, who had a pitch at Charing Cross station, recalled how he had picked up a small piece of rolled up paper which had been thrown out of a taxi-cab window. Unbelievably, it turned out to be the left luggage receipt for the trunk – which at last gave them the deposit date. This led Cornish on to trace the cabbie who had carried the trunk to the station from the doorway of a block of offices near Westminster Police Court.

The trunk had been heavy.

'What have you got in there – money?' the cabbie had joked.

'No, it's books' the fare replied.

It turned out that the trunk had been noticed by everyone who worked in the office block but they were no help. However, there *was* a set of empty offices in the block which bore the notice, *Edwards & Co, Estate Business Transfer Agents*. The offices had been hired by a Mr John Robinson who, on 9 May, the day *before* the discovery of the trunk, had written to the landlord informing him that he had to let the offices go as he had gone broke. Seemed like this might be another dead end?

Luckily, the cheque by which John Robinson had paid the landlord, led to his bank and, although he had gone from his given address, a returned telegram found there led to his *current* address where two officers waited for him to show up so they could invite him to Scotland Yard. An invitation to which, Wensley recalled, 'He readily agreed.'

It turned out that John Robinson was a man of many parts which he described 'with great plausibility'. First, he had been a Blackpool tram conductor, then a greengrocer, a bookmaker, a milkman, and a soldier but, most frequently, a pub barman. He had been married in Ireland, 'bigamously we found out' but 'there was nothing in his appearance or manner to suggest a man who would commit cold-blooded murder'.

'Few people realise,' Wensley commented when relating this tale, 'the amount of work that is involved in any complicated murder investigation'.[2]

In this, case it had been nine days since the discovery of the body and they had hit a brick wall again. A conference of all concerned resulted in several other steps being taken. One being the re-examination of Robinson's former offices which was carried out by a couple of 'enthusiastic and painstaking detective sergeants, Clarke and Burt'.

Little seemed to have been overlooked in the initial search. Nonetheless, they gave everything a thorough checking this time including minutely examining the contents of a wastepaper basket full of scraps of paper, cigarette stubs and burnt matches. Each scrap was carefully perused and, Clarke noticed, one match was discoloured and, taking it closer to the light, realised that it was bloodstained.

Fortunately, back in 1901, scientists had at last discovered both how to differentiate between animal blood and human blood *and* to develop the first system of blood grouping but not, of course to pinpoint the person from who it came. Nonetheless, this was a great breakthrough.

Another breakthrough occurred when the duster which had been wrapped around the head, and had now been cleaned, revealed the word *Greyhound* in one corner. This was traced to the Greyhound Hotel where Robinson had worked, as did the girl he had bigamously married and *she* had taken the duster to the offices.

Robinson denied ever having seen any trunk in the entrance to the offices or having any knowledge of Mrs Bonati but 'quite nonchalantly and cheerfully' agreed to go to the cabman and the trunk salesman to see whether they could identify him. He was in luck. Neither man could and Cornish let him go.

On the very day when a newspaper announced the police were 'baffled' by the case, Robinson was again invited to the Yard where, this time, he decided to tell Cornish 'all about it'.

There are two reasons why this scenario so often occurs. Guilty suspects become exhausted by all the effort of worrying, lying and prevaricating and/or they overestimate how much evidence the police already have against them. It's a lonely situation and they want someone to share their burden – by telling them their version of events.

Robinson now told them he had fallen in with a strange woman at Victoria Station and she had suggested coming back to his offices with him where she sat while he wrote some letters then told him she was hard up and asked him for a pound. He refused and she fell into a rage and became abusive. Again, we have the innocent man and a woman initiating the aggression.

'She bent down, as though to pick something up from the fireplace and came towards me. I hit her on the face with my right hand . . . She fell backwards, struck her head on a chair, ending up with her head in the fireplace. 'I left her there and came out, closing the office door behind me.' Then he went home, as you would.

Next day, he was surprised to find her still there – and dead. Then followed the story of cutting up the body – with a knife bought at the same shop which Mahon had patronised for a similar purpose. But medical experts disagreed with his version of events saying that Mrs Bonati's bruises told a different story. After a struggle she had become unconscious, they said, and then had been deliberately suffocated with a soft cushion or something similar. Robinson was charged with murder, found guilty and hanged.

The following year saw the opening of one of the most outstanding murder enquiries Scotland Yard dealt with during the 1920s – at least from the point of view of the shock the crime caused and the effort and determination put into the solving. The story began at six in the morning of 27 September, 1927, when a mail van driver found the body of an Essex Constabulary Policeman on the side of a quiet country road near Stapleford Abbot.

Constable Gutteridge, a steady, middle-aged, happily-married man, had obviously been about to record some details in his notebook which lay nearby, the pencil still clutched in his hand. His helmet lay nearby. He had been shot four times in the head, twice at very close range – into his eyes. There were car tyre marks on the near side of the road close to the verge.

Scotland Yard were immediately called in and taking charge

was the bearded and moustachioed Chief Inspector Berrett, who had the appearance of a gentleman farmer. No effort was to be spared. This was the cold-blooded murder of one of their own.

Given the rural constable's background the idea of a revenge or jealousy murder was quickly dismissed. What was more likely, in the light of the increase in motor car theft by armed criminals and the fact that Essex bordered on London, was that Gutteridge may have stopped a suspicious looking vehicle to check up on it.

The Crime Index at Scotland Yard was duly consulted. A likely list of motor bandits prone to violence was compiled and the tracking down began. Some suspects were found and eliminated. Some could not be traced.

An early very promising possibility was an ex-convict who had been released after serving 15 years for the manslaughter of a Lancashire constable. In addition, he had recently committed an offence in nearby Billericay, which was not far from the scene of the crime. Better still, a bloodstained bandage and newspapers describing the Gutteridge murder were found in his rooms and he had not slept at home on the night in question. Alas, his claim that he had spent that night in a night club was verified. He had a watertight alibi.

Shortly after the murder, a clerk living in the Brixton suburb noticed a Morris-Cowley four-seater car parked in the cul-de-sac at the back of his house. The radiator was still warm and the car was still there the next morning so he informed the police. They found that the left front wing was bent, the running board bore splashes of what was later to be found to be blood and an empty cartridge found under the driver's seat was of the same calibre as those which had killed Constable Gutteridge. Moreover, the car proved to belong to a Dr Lovell of Billericay and it had been stolen from his garage at around 2.30am on the night of the murder. The doctor had left some medical instruments in his car which gave the police something else with which to identify the suspects – once they were found.

Meanwhile, back at the Yard, the cartridge case was recognised by Assistant Commissioner Childs, a man with considerable army experience, as a type withdrawn soon after the outbreak of the war. He also noticed that the wounds showed that one of the bullets had been propelled by a black powder not used since 1894.

There were three months without any progress despite the *News of the World* doubling its reward for any information to £2,000. Then, Sheffield City Police reported that one of their chief suspects, Frederick Guy Browne, was back at his old habits of stealing motor cars so, on 27 January, 1928, they decided to raid his garage. Dr Lovell identified some of the medical equipment which had been in his stolen car but Browne denied anything to do with the Gutteridge murder even though one of his Webley handguns produced the same peculiar mark on a cartridge case as the one used that night.

Patrick Kennedy, the man who had been with Browne that night, was identified and found. Browne continued to deny any involvement but Kennedy eventually admitted having been present at the scene but that Browne had done all the shooting. He had been shocked and terrified by the man's actions which caused him to reload his own revolver. He described how Browne, having shot Gutteridge from inside the car, jumped out saying, 'I'll finish the bugger!' and leaned over the dying man exclaiming, 'What are you looking at me like that for!' and shot him in the eyes.

Unfortunately for Kennedy, an expert claimed that the bullets which killed Gutteridge had been fired from two *different* weapons and he had not gone into the witness box to give *his* version of events.

Both men were found guilty and hanged. The case received a great deal of attention at the time not because it was the murder of an unarmed policeman but also that he had been shot in the eyes due, it was presumed, to the superstition that the last thing a dying man sees is recorded in his eyes.

When musing on murder generally Wensley thought that it may be equally well committed because a man was hard and determined or weak and irresolute but, curiously, that *most* suspects objected to being thought of as murderers. 'They will admit that they intended to 'kill' but not that they intended to 'murder.'[3]

Whatever their mental capacity those with murder in mind would have been reminded that you are less likely to get away with it if you kill a policeman.

P C Gutteridge's murder remains a very well-known one in police history. In September, 2019, the Chief Constable of Norfolk where the constable was born, and the Parish Council of the actual village, Wimbotsham, decided to commemorate Gutteridge's life with a brass plaque showing his uniformed photograph and a storyboard describing his life and awful death.

NOTES FOR CHAPTER NINE

1. *Detective Days* by Frederick Porter Wensley, p248-258
2. *Ibid,* p248
3. *Ibid* p270

10
Getting Booked

Unsurprisingly, echoes of the real-life murder appeared in the Golden Age detective novels some obviously so, as in *The Poisoned Chocolates Case* by Anthony Berkeley[1], others merely emerged in plots, characters, themes and backgrounds. Thus, the shade of Edith Thompson and Herbert Rouse Armstrong hovered and venues like The Crumbles came once again into view – this time as The Jumbles[2].

Other Golden Age authors gazed well back in time to such as The Staffordshire Palmer Poisonings of 1856 in which, interestingly, a private detective involved was Charles Frederick Field who had been one of Scotland Yard's very first detectives. As such, he had escorted Charles Dickens around the seamier side of London which was not always easily accessed even by the author on his celebrated walks. Field was believed to be a template for Inspector Bucket in *Bleak House* although Dickens denied this, possibly because Field was an embarrassing self-publicist[3].

Many real-life murder stories also were related by the real-life police detectives who had actually handled the cases for, they too, wrote books, both autobiographies and on crime in general and had done so since late Victorian times.[4] The detectives were very famous men, and eagerly read having become well-known after being mentioned by name many times in the newspaper reports about crimes they were handling.

The detectives also featured in various newspaper articles and series in which they related their exploits. Now and then, warnings about these practices were issued, pointing out the provisions of the Official Secrets Act and the Police Pensions Act under which they could be prosecuted for revealing confidential information and withdrawal of pension was threatened if such articles and books were found to be objectionable. Indeed, in 1861, Field's pension had been stopped for six months because he insisted on giving the impression that he was still a police detective when, in fact, was now operating as a private enquiry agent.

A detective who became aware of the risks of writing about his exploits was John Sweeney, one of the Irishmen who landed up in Special Branch due to the IRA threat. He was sued by one Luigi Parmegianni for alleging that not only was Luigi a notorious anarchist, but also a receiver of stolen goods. After bringing several witnesses – civilian and police – to back him up, Sweeney was found not guilty of the former but guilty of the latter accusation, though fined only a farthing.[5]

Another police officer had even written detective novels. He was Superintendent Frank Castle Froest, the first head of the official Murder Squad in 1907. In uniform the thick-set Froest was described as looking like a Prussian Field Marshal. Out of it, he was immaculate and had 'all the appearance of a prosperous and ingenuous country gentleman.'[6] Some of Froests's novels were written in partnership with true crime writer George Dilnot but two of his own, *The Grell Mystery* and *The Maelstrom*, were made into films in 1917.

However, his own police duty exploits were worthy of fiction. In 1895, while a detective inspector, the multilingual Froest had been told to go to Argentina and not come back without the super-embezzler Jabez Spencer Balfour who had fled there leaving his investors short of around six million pounds – a colossal sum at that time.[7] Whilst other Scotland Yard men already out there were negotiating his extradition Balfour had fled a thousand miles up-country to Salta in the foothills of the Andes where he was being protected by cronies.

Froest went up to Salta, for a supposedly official handover due to take place the next day before the train went back to Buenos Aires. But the timing allowed for more crony interference so Froest hired another train and had the armed British Console guard Balfour, whilst *he* rode on the footplate. A sheriff's posse rode out to intercept them further down the line but Froest covered the driver with the pistol to keep him driving the train. Unfortunately, whilst attempting to board the train, a Sheriff's Officer was killed falling from his horse.

Further battles took place *en route* but they eventually made it back to the Argentinian capitol and on to London where Balfour was sentenced to 14 years penal servitude and the exploit made Froest famous.

In the 1920s the first Scotland Yard detective out of the autobiography starting-block (following his retirement in 1926) was the dapper, fastidious, Superintendent Francis Carlin, with his *Reminiscences of an Ex-Detective*.

Unlike some other police auto-biographers Carlin did not

start by offering a snapshot of his early life before he joined. He merely informed us that his father had been a constable in London's Camden Town and that conditions were very different now. Then came the brief details of his first days in some rough venues such as Limehouse where physical abuse of young constables by the locals was not unusual.

Then it was on to Bow Street which covered the then glamorous theatreland of The Strand and the murky dens of Seven Dials. As with many of his senior colleagues, he had made it into the CID quite early, then risen rapidly. Thus came brief stories of his successes as a thief catcher while on the beat which were clearly due to his enthusiasm, observation and diligence. In some cases this classic route could have a dark side.

(According to London Magistrate's Clerk, F T Giles, this golden pathway could lead less scrupulous officers to trump up offences, particularly with the aid of the charge of 'Being a Suspected Person' which needed only the officer's evidence to prove. Giles called it the most dangerous charge in English Criminal Law and described just such a case in his book *Open Court*.[8])

Carlin had joined in 1890, aged nineteen. His first posting after joining had been to K Division (which included the very rough Limehouse district) at the time of the dock strike. His first attempt to capture a criminal had earned him an attack from a gang who knocked him out. By 1898 he was a detective sergeant 2nd Class and his keenness and application was aptly demonstrated when, soon after his promotion, he was given the task of tracing a Midlands solicitor who had absconded with a large sum of money left in trust for a brother and sister.

So as not to alert the man's friends Carlin had carried a small samples case to the Midlands town, thus giving the impression that he was a travelling salesman, so was able to discover that his quarry had left for London where he was staying in a particular hotel. But he found the bird had flown from there – leaving at 2pm which, the young sergeant deduced, may mean he was heading for the 2.20pm express to Boulogne. He followed, contacting one of the Yard men posted at the port and, with his and local police help, managed to peruse the Boulogne Hotel registers.

Obviously, the suspect would not use his own name but Carlin had acquainted himself with knowledge of the names peculiar to certain districts: Robson on Tyneside; Dunnett in Suffolk; Chidgey in Somerset and so on. Seeing a Midlands name beginning with a W, which he knew was peculiar to the Midlands District from which his quarry came, he showed the solicitor's photo and it was confirmed that this was his man – who had just sailed for America.

He informed his chiefs that he was certain that the absconding solicitor was heading for New York. They sent off a cable asking for the man to be detained on arrival. They received a reply saying he *had* been, but was denying the identification. This, Carlin recalled, caused a fluttering in the dovecotes which was allayed a couple of days later when another cable announced, 'Man admits his identity.'

Carlin was sent over to collect the solicitor from New York's Tombs Prison. On return the two men became friends and when he was asked if 'his uncle' would take the chair at the ship's concert, Carlin agreed and even offered to sing a song himself. On arrival back home his 'uncle' got five years and

Carlin an early boost to his career.

By 1916 he was one of the five Detective Chief Inspectors in charge at Scotland Yard alongside Wensley, Fowler, Gough and Hawkins, and it was the name of a case he handled during that first year: *The Eltham Common Murder* with which he titled his book's first chapter. Next came *Breaking Up a Gang of Daring Forgers* followed by *The Berkeley Hotel Robbery* and so on. For, of course, murder cases were not their bread and butter as was the diet of the fictional detective.

Like his colleagues he was well aware that in detective fiction the police were often portrayed as inept blunderers compared with their upper-class, educated, amateur sleuths. In the first of his two chapters on *Methods of the Scotland Yard Men,* he tackles the subject thus:

'Let me first take the query which has most often been propounded to me. It is this: Are the methods of the real-life detectives at all like those of the detectives of fiction?'

He then points out that, in fiction the sleuth who always got his man was allowed 350-400 pages in which to do so whilst *they* must often get him quickly or not at all. He then describes their official methods at murder scenes explaining that, while fingerprints *were* very useful in identifying *known* criminals and their modus operandi, murder was often a one-off affair so they were less likely to find those of the suspect in their fingerprint files.

The detective story scribes were listening. Ernest Bramah, had been writing about his blind super-sleuth, Max Carrados, since 1914. Come his 1927 outing, *The Holloway Flat Tragedy,* in which the hugely convoluted plot begins with the murderer posing as the victim seeking protection against himself is finally brought to justice when, says Carrados, 'Crispinge furnished us with a solitary fingerprint that linked up his identity'.

'He had been convicted then?' responds his 'Watson'.

'Blackmail, six years ago, and other things before.'[9]

Among the several sets of Rules compiled by commentators and writers the use of disguise came up. In *his* set of rules, T.S. Elliot decreed that disguise should only be occasional and incidental.[10] When Carlin was asked whether Scotland Yard made use of them his answer was an emphatic 'No!'

Then he went on to admit that he had often used what he called 'character disguises' such as dressing the part of a shop walker, a navvy, a sailor, or a professional man just changing his speech and manner to fit. 'But my face remained unaltered. You must fit into your background. It would scarcely be effective, for instance to enter the lounge of the Ritz Hotel disguised as a Chinese sailor.'

You might take that as 'a qualified no' but of course in those days there were substantial differences in the way people dressed – according to class, work, situation, etc. Nowadays even a Lord wears jeans.

One of the most effective 'disguises' Carlin had ever seen was used by a detective who dressed as a uniformed constable so that he could wander past a gang of thieves who were meeting in Covent Garden and listen to their conversation. The thieves barely glanced at him. 'For how should they suspect a 'dull headed, stolid bobby'.

As for the deductive or inductive methods of investigation which Sherlock Holmes went on about to 'that obtuse but long-suffering satellite Watson' *his* colleagues had always favoured the deductive method and *this* was also one of the chief differences between Scotland Yard and the detective systems of other countries.

Fortunately, he then describes the *differences* between these two methods. The inductive method caused the detective to *assume* one or more things. Then he worked, out of his experience of crimes and criminals, to *confirm these assumptions*. This, indeed, was the chief characteristic of the Parisian detective and, whilst that might be suitable to the laws of France, it might easily lead the English detective into trouble.

Scotland Yard worked with 'less brilliance but more security'. Therefore, they found the deductive method safer. They began with the *clues* then deduced inferences from *them*.

(In fact, following the 1870s Scotland Yard corruption scandal, some French organisational methods had been adopted by the Yard.)

He wasn't saying they *never* used induction. When there were no clues the detective might well consult the Criminal Records Office for particular techniques used or, 'to use everyday slang, he must occasionally 'chance his arm'.

He then gave over a whole chapter on *The Psychology of the Criminal*. There was, Carlin declared, no such thing as 'the criminal type' despite what phrenologists and physiognomist might say. However, *all* criminals were lazy, gamblers, spendthrifts and very vain – the latter being a besetting weakness. The average criminal was also singularly unintelligent. Strong proof of this was that they were extremely imitative and incapable of sustained effort – which was very helpful to the police. The exceptions were the master criminals such as swindlers, forgers and confidence tricksters who treated crime like a business and often kept out of the line of fire.

As for identifying a criminal by his personal appearance; 'I would lay it down that only among the lower order of criminals – and in these, even, it is rapidly disappearing – do you find the close-set eyes, the broad-set nose widening at the nostrils, the pointed low-set ears, and the brutal jowl which people once used to classify as the criminal type.'

To show he had done his homework Carlin dropped in the names of most of the prominent writers and thinkers on criminology and psychiatry: Lombroso, Freud, Jung, Von Kraft Ebbing and Havelock Ellis. Despite including the last two he left the analysis of sexual offenders to them but included them when stating the two main *causes* of crime were 'laziness and lust'.

From further down the detective ranks came the book *Crooks and Crime* (1928) by former Detective Inspector J Kenneth Ferrier who had done such a sterling PR job for The Yard at the 1904 St Louis Exhibition when describing our fingerprinting classification method.

As the title indicates, his book is more about the criminals and their methods from cardsharpers to blackmailers, burglars and coiners meanwhile revealing some interesting insider knowledge such as that cardsharpers polish both sides of the court cards (Kings, Queens and Aces) so that they slip out readily when dealing and that they sprinkled 'the rags' with the dust of resin to make them 'sluggish'. Also, that a sharper who had a particularly sensitive touch could identify the court cards in a new pack by pressing it against a table. This was because manufacturers used a refined gum to protect larger areas of colour and this made them stick to the card beneath them. All useful knowledge at a time when, post war, so many wealthy potential dupes were flooding into the country.

Coining was not that difficult, he said, but the passing of the false coins *was* and women were very often used to 'accidentally' do this but to be successful must offer only one coin at a time.

Ferrier also thought the modern confidence man was 'the prince of crooks'. To be successful he needed the qualities of an actor and the nerves of an acrobat together with colossal impudence, agreeable manners, a glib and persuasive tongue and a good knowledge of psychology and geography. He must also possess a ready wit and an inventive mind which was never flustered and a full measure of *sang froid*. Apparently, the man who possessed all these traits was the Australian George Smith 'the confidence man supreme' who had left the dock a free man after Ferrier had first charged him but, within a year, he was back and, this time, left with a police escort.[11]

As to the influx of the con men's typical victims since the end of the war (wealthy Americans and Colonials longing to enjoy the delights of Europe once again) the Yard had been charged with catching the men who preyed on them. DI Charles Leach relates being instructed to form a squad to combat the problem.

In *his* book, *On Top of the Underworld* (1933), Leach describes entering a famous café and seeing over twenty or thirty of the cleverest International con men sitting at various tables around the room. Few of them were English, most being Australian or Americans with a few Frenchmen and the odd Spaniard mixed in. All were well-travelled, elegant but not ostentatious. Had they not managed to ingratiate themselves with 'a mark' whilst on the liner or train *en route* they would haunt London sights and the lounges of the best hotels, presenting themselves as wealthy stockbrokers, racehorse owners, retired cattle farmers or gold miners or simply gentlemen of leisure.[12] Amongst themselves they were known by apt nicknames: 'Dictionary Harry, Cut-Face, Dave the Liar, Pretty Sid, Chicago Solly, The Count, Australian Jack' etc.[13]

Most of their deceptions centred around can't-lose bets, sure-fire investments and rigged card games and one of the greatest difficulties for police was to get the mark to charge the offender when caught. However outraged initially, most of them felt too embarrassed to let the world know how easily they had been duped. Leach found that while under the spell of the conman the victims could be so excited by the prospect of easy money that it was often difficult or even impossible to save them from themselves.

One of Leach's team, D I Percy J. Smith, was *also* later to write a book simply called *Con Man,* in which he describes such a failure. After seeing an American guest in company with a well-known trickster named Davidson, a hotel manager alerted the local police who sent over two detectives. But the con man had left, only a quiet friend remained, so the detectives had a chat with the American warning him of the dangers. But the advice was far from welcome. The man resented the intrusion in his personal affairs and insisted he had not entered into any business deal with Davidson nor drawn out any large sums of money recently.

What the detectives did *not* know was that the quiet friend was *also* a con man. Neither was it true that no withdrawals had been made. Indeed, five thousand pounds were sitting in the pocket of the dupe even as they spoke. As soon as the officers left the quiet friend suddenly jumped to his feet declaring that 'the tecs' were imposters, most likely *they* were trying to relieve them of their cash. *He was* going to make sure that *his* was in a place of safety.

The pair hurriedly took a cab to Selfridges where 'the friend' told the American to hold the taxi while he put his £10,000 into his safety deposit box. The now-frightened dupe exclaimed 'Here, take mine as well.' The quiet friend went in the front door of Selfridges and straight out of the back. It was 'a sad and chastened man' who later told Inspector Smith the story.[14]

If con men were the admired crooks, at least for their talent, blackmailers were the most despised in the eyes of the CID – possibly because *they* were more likely to be faced with the distressed victims.

Ferrier thought this crime the most vicious, vile, and villainous; 'and more contemptible than cheating at cards' (surely, an odd comparison). The blackmailer was 'a bloodsucking, despicable wretch who lived on the moral weakness of his victim'. He described many such cases – all of which concerned heterosexual matters in which either the husband or wife had transgressed but gives no space to those involving male homosexuals who, at the time of course, were *more* vulnerable as such acts were illegal.[15]

Unsurprisingly, Ferrier made much of the value of fingerprints and related several British and US experiences in which they had proved not just guilt but innocence. Alas, although he did not mention it, at the time fingerprint identification system was suffering severe setback due to a) The Sheppard Inquiry and b) the Yard's changes in handling prints.

The Sheppard Inquiry was the result of the mistaken

identity arrest of Major R O Sheppard and his subsequent handling at Vine Street Police Station during which, he claimed, his human rights had been violated. This included the taking of his fingerprints without his permission.

The police knew that old lags would be laughing up their sleeves because this so-called reform would operate in their favour and to the detriment of the public. Formerly, when an arrest was made, fingerprints were taken as a matter of course.

Until then, if the accused refused to have them taken, police could obtain them via an order signed by a magistrate authorising them to be taken by the prison authorities *after* the accused had been remanded in custody. Now, they could not. A huge setback.

Chief Inspector Charles Arrow claimed that he had never known a prisoner object to the practice but now that they had the opportunity of declining they naturally did so.[16]

As for Scotland Yard's own hiccup (from 1923 to 1925 only seventy crimes had been solved due to fingerprint identification). This appeared to be largely due to their new Single Fingerprint filing system. To simplify and quicken searches it was decided to file each digit in a separate file but clearly this wasn't working very well. DCI Harry Battley. the new head of department, set out to refine the process adding more means of identification. Subsequently, 1928-9 saw a sharp rise of successes to three hundred and sixty.

However, in England and Wales the results of the Sheppard 'reform' lasted until the Criminal Justice Act of 1948.

Fred Cherrill, who became head of the bureau in 1939, pointed out how the work of the police might be greatly hampered by their inability to obtain the prints of a person under arrest when needed to compare with fingerprints found at the scene of a crime.[17]

After 1948, if an accused refused his prints they could be taken nonetheless *if* he had appeared before court and by the order of an inspector or above. Better, but still hampering justice.

NOTES FOR CHAPTER TEN

1. *The Poisoned Chocolates Case*, by Anthony Berkeley, 1929. A group of six society intellectuals think they will succeed in solving who sent the poisoned chocolates to womanising cad, Sir Eustace, where police have failed. Readers are offered six solutions.

2. *The Jumbles:* a murder scene in *The Scoop*, a Detection Club round-robin story for the BBC; *The Golden Age of Murder* (2015), p169.

3. When I went in search of Field's grave in Brompton Road the cemetery was so overgrown that two visits were needed, the second armed with a grave map. And there it was – a grand plinth which announced that D I Field had been a *Chief* Detective Inspector. Still telling fibs!

4. See in Bibliographies of Victorian non-fiction crime books.

5. *Scotland Yard Casebook, p183.*

6. *Sunday News*, 12 January, 1930; *The Times, 8 January, 1930 (obituary).*

7. Assistant Commissioner Sir Robert Anderson, who sent Froest out to Argentina, gleefully relates this tale in his *The Lighter Side of My Official Life* (1910) while adding 'the relatives of the unfortunate sheriff's officer received compensation for

his death'. It is related more fully by George Dilnot in *Scotland Yard* (1929).

8. *Open Court,* p92-96.

9. *Capital Crimes,* p116

10. *The Golden Age of Murder, p113*

11. *Crooks and Crime, p139*

12. *On Top of the Underworld, p155-6*

13. *Con Man, p41*

14. *Ibid, p11-15*

15. *Crooks and Crime,* p170

16. *Rogues and Others,* p223

17. *Cherrill of the Yard, p102*

11

The Garage Murders

Of course, the purpose of the detective novel was entertainment. Not really meant to be taken that seriously by the readers. Just good fun. Therefore writers must not try to outsmart them by cheating. Not being fair.

In his preface to *Best Detective Stories of 1928-29* Ronald Knox enlightened them by explaining how they might bring that about with his ten rules to help achieve this equality between the fictional tec and the reader.

For example, though 'the criminal must be someone mentioned in the early part of the story, but must not be anyone whose thoughts the reader has been allowed to follow.' (Which makes it a bit tricky if you are writing in the first person singular.)

Nothing supernatural is allowed and nor more than one secret room or passage. According to crime writer Robert Barnard this rule prevented 'contamination from the Gothic'.[1]

'No hitherto undiscovered poisons may be used, nor any appliance which will need a long scientific explanation at the end.' Obviously *both* would be unfair, as the reader would have no chance of spotting their presence.

'No accident must ever help the detective nor must he ever have an unaccountable intuition which proves to be right' – again you are not playing fair with the reader if you don't allow them to be privy to all the investigative aids.

'No Chinaman must figure in the story' – sinister oriental villains such as Fu Manchu had become racist clichés in thrillers.

The detective must not commit the crime and 'must not light upon any clues which are not instantly produced for the inspection of the reader' – obviously again – not fair. Similarly, no twins or doubles – 'unless we have been duly prepared for them'.

And, finally, 'The stupid friend of the detective, the Watson, must not conceal any thoughts which pass through his mind; his intelligence must be slightly, but very slightly, below that of the average reader' – which, of course, doesn't say much for Knox's opinion of detective novel readers.

But, as Martin Edwards points out, Knox didn't expect his rules to be taken all that seriously. 'He would have been amazed, as well as amused, to find so many commentators in later years taking his jokes at face value.' [2]

Although no real murders occurred in country houses nor amongst the intellectual elite during the late Twenties and much of the crime being dealt with by Scotland Yard detectives tended to centre around the more mundane crimes such as burglary, nonetheless, these could throw up some complex murder cases. For example, *The Pembridge Square Murder* which Divisional Detective Inspector John E Horwell was called upon to solve in February, 1928.

Horwell's parents had kept a small shop in Hackney and he

had attended the local board school which he had left at aged thirteen. After joining the Metropolitan Police in 1905 he made it to the CID four years later as a detective constable but his lack of formal education made his climb up the following ranks hard, particularly since passing civil service as well as police exams was now necessary. It wasn't until 1925, via intensive study at evening classes that Horwell made it to the rank of Detective Inspector in charge of a large chunk of West London CID which had its headquarters at Paddington Police Station.

The murder he was called upon to solve in February, 1928, was seemingly simple but complicated by the fact that there appeared to be no connection between the victim and possible suspects. A uniformed constable had rung in to say that he had been called to a large house in Pembridge Square, Notting Hill, which had been turned into luxury flats. There, he had found a gentleman lying on the stairs outside his first floor flat with a bullet wound in his head. He had died shortly afterwards.

A glass panel in his front door had been smashed and Horwell quickly realised that this was probably the work of 'an afternoon flat-breaker'. The premises had been ransacked by an expert thief. Empty jewel cases and drawer contents were strewn about the floor. Just inside the door lay an envelope face down, marked with blood – indicating that the thief probably cut his hand whilst reaching through the broken glass. Having heard Webb trying to open the door, then seen him peering through the broken glass, he had shot him in the forehead causing him to fall backwards down the stairs.

However, there *was* a witness. Webb and his son had returned home at about 6pm and when he had seen the damaged door, he realised that his flat had been entered and told his son to run for a policeman. As the son did so, he heard a shot, then a short, dark man pushed past him and ran out of the house disappearing into the fog. Fortunately, a passing woman *also* saw the man and noticed his hand shoot out as though throwing something away. This turned out to be a small automatic pistol found in one of the gardens.

Experience taught Horwell that this was doubtless the work of 'a drummer' – a thief who knocks on doors until he is greeted by silence but, if someone answers, he asks for Mr Smith or Jones or some other fictional person. Horwell organised a thorough house to house search of the whole of Bayswater area to find anyone who had answered such a knock and meanwhile pulled in thieves known for this type of crime. Alas, all had alibis, and Horwell, well aware (even in those days) of the need to make progress during the first twenty-four hours, was becoming despondent. Then, on the sixth day, he was relieved to find a lady who *had* answered such a knock to a short, dark, stocky man who said, 'I should like to see the chauffer, madam.'

She had asked him where he came from and, after a slight hesitation, he had replied, 'Warwick Garage.'

The lady told him she had no chauffeur and was not expecting anyone from the garage so he apologised and left. Spirits rose when she was able to provide quite a good description of the man but, although this was sent to police countrywide, it was not recognised, and 'Warwick Garage' proved not to exist. Stalemate.

The gun was not what Horwell termed 'a man stopper' but the fact that a second bullet had jammed in the barrel indicated that the killer had mean business. Horwell took the unusual step of holding 'a war conference' – getting everyone involved in the enquiry to talk freely about their ideas and impressions – and kept asking them if they could throw any light on the words 'Warwick Garage'.

Suddenly, a detective sergeant offered, 'there is a flat-breaker named Stewart who used to hang about in the neighbourhood of Warwick Mews in Kensington.' Acting on the presumption that the thief may have said the first place which came into his head – 'Warwick' – then added 'Garage', the team were instructed to drop everything else whilst they sought out this 'Stewart'. They learned that he was a regular race-goer: flat racing when in season – which it was not – and dog racing in the evenings.

Horwell reasoned that Stewart would *not* chance *London* dog races while the heat was on but that those in Southend were not too far away . . . He sent a sergeant who knew Stewart down to that popular seaside resort. Later, the same day, he received a phone call to say that Stewart was in a cell at Southend Police Station having been caught in a pub next to the dog-racing track and been taken in fighting and struggling.

Stewart admitted to having been the burglar but denied that he was a murderer. He claimed it had been an accident. When realising he had been caught, he had made a dash through the door with his jemmy under his left arm and his pistol in his right hand. As he did so, the man outside (Mr Webb, the flat owner) had struck him on the back of the neck. This had sent him reeling backwards with his arms upwards. As he fell, his pistol fired. It had been an accident and it would not have happened if the man had not struck him with such force.

So it was Mr Webb's own fault – a scenario with which neither Horwell, the pathologist, nor the jury, agreed. He was found Guilty of Murder and hanged on Derby Day which was an event Stewart had not missed for many years.[3]

Coincidentally, Pembridge Square was also to play a big part in my life as it was in a woman police section house (formed out of three of the square's houses) that I lived for a couple of years after I joined the Metropolitan Police in 1954.

The locked room mystery was a Golden Age detective novel speciality. The principle of the puzzle being how the killer got in and out of the (locked room) crime scene without being caught or leaving any clues. Fans of such specialities may have salivated had they read the message received by Scotland Yard from the Chief Constable of Southampton on 10 January, 1929. It read:

A case of murder has occurred here. A man has been found shot dead in a room the door of which was padlocked. The body was found today and has probably been in the room for some eight or nine weeks. Will you please send an officer down to investigate the matter.[4]

Of course, this probably did *not* qualify as a *genuine* locked room mystery since the lock was already there on the outside. All that was needed was the key.

This time it was the turn of the tall, commanding, and immaculately-dressed, Chief Inspector John Prothero to answer the summons to aid the force of this busy port city. With him, he took Highland Scot, Sergeant Hugh Young.

No-one could accuse the local police with undue early interference with this crime scene. Rather the reverse. Over two months before the victim, Vivian Messiter, had been reported missing to the local police by his landlord. They had duly sent a police officer to Messiter's garage/storeroom which had been found securely locked so, it was concluded, that wherever Messiter was, he wasn't there.

The landlord (an ex-policeman) then wrote to Wolf's Head Oil, reporting their local agent missing. They asked the landlord to visit the garage, which he did, broke a window and peering in, saw that the missing man's car was still in situ but that there appeared to be nothing amiss. Therefore, *he* presumed that Messiter must have just left – possibly returning to the United States where he had lived for some time.

The missing man had last been seen on 30 October and, on 10 January, Wolf's Head Oil sent a replacement, a Mr Passmore, who gained access to the outer yard over the roof of the next-door pub then broke into the garage. Inside, he found Messiter's body face-up amongst a pile of boxes and oil drums. Unsurprisingly, it was very decomposed. There was a small round hole in his forehead and the rats had been at his face.

Initially, the hole caused police to conclude that he had been shot. But heavy blood splashing, a blood-stained hammer and an examination by Spilsbury established that he had in fact been brutally bludgeoned to death.

Local police handed over a duplicate order book and memorandum book from which pages had been torn. Amongst them was a receipt signed by a Mr H H Galton on 30 October, 1928, – the last day Messiter was seen alive. Also, just discernable on two sheets of carbon paper was a name and address: Cromer & Bartlett, Bold Street, Southampton – then a couple of notes – *Sold to Ben Baskerfield, Clayton Farm, Bentley Road near Winchester and Ben Jervis, Crescent Bassett, 5 gallons number 8 at 5s6d.*

Since the crime scene had not been disturbed, Prothero arranged a re-enactment of the murder, local police persuading the next door licensee to stand in for Messiter. Sergeant Young placed his hat beside the landlord's head to take the place of Messiter's trilby which had been found there. Then Prothero ordered a thorough search of the garage. A couple of discarded scraps of paper referring to an order and a meeting with a Mr W F Thomas were found. In Messiter's lodgings was found the reply to his advertisement in the local paper – from a W F Thomas.

There followed a projected search for Thomas, extended whilst the Wiltshire Police were pursuing him for £130 wages theft committed on a building firm to which he had applied for a job just after he had left Southampton. A scrap of paper found in his lodgings *there* led on to Manchester where the police wanted him – under the name of Podmore – for another offence. It was a year before Prothero had Thomas/Podmore back which gave him time to build up a watertight case against him built on the presumption that Podmore had been cheating Messiter with fake claims, been challenged, and so killed the man.

Podmore was an experienced thief and liar but one of the matters which finally tripped him up was the fact that he interwove his lies with names or addresses which he clearly had recalled from around his home in Staffordshire: Bold Street, Clayton Farm, Ben Jervis, Cromer & Bartlett and Baskerfield.

As with Stewart in the Pembridge Square murder these were familiar names which obviously had just popped up in his head automatically.

He was found Guilty and hanged.[5]

*   *   *

Occasionally, one of the London murders had more than a touch of the exotic about them such as the one which emerged on an August evening in 1929. Two young constables were patrolling the Outer Circle of Regent's Park when they heard unmistakably human cries coming from the direction of London Zoo's Tapir House then spotted a man lying at the foot of the thick privet hedge between the House and the Zoo's outer railings.

The constables vaulted over the railings and went to the man's aid. He was making incoherent remarks but they began to understand that he had jumped from his bedroom above the Tapir House and that another man, who shared the bedroom, was still in there badly injured and that they had been attacked by several men.

The constables managed to alert the Zoo Superintendent and his assistant. The injured man was, in fact, an elephant trainer from Burma by the name of San Dwe or, popularly, Sandy Wee. His roommate was the famous elephant trainer, Said Ali, who was Indian.

'He is finished,' Sandy Wee declared. 'Four men killed him.'

The young policemen found that the door to the bedroom had been smashed in and Said Ali was lying dead in his bed from ferocious wounds caused by a sledgehammer and a pickaxe.

The case went to Divisional D I Walter Hambrook who, at the time, had just returned from his holiday.

'I at once motored to the Zoo,' he recalled in his autobiography. There, he found that a terrible struggle had taken place which seemed to confirm Sandy Wee's statement that four men had burst through the front door. The pickaxe blade fitted the indentations – but there were bloodstains on these marks. 'Which, at once aroused our suspicions.'

Sandy Wee explained that Said Ali had been out doing some shopping, returned at about 9.30pm, then had sat by the bedroom window looking out over the Outer Circle roadway. He had drawn Sandy Wee's attention to some noisy people in the road saying, 'They are like animals.'

Two Englishmen in the road had overheard him and shouted, 'Shut up, you black man! Shut up!'

Sandy Wee then went to sleep to be woken up by Said Ali calling out, 'Who are you?' Then four men were hitting Said.

'I take some of my blankets and jump out of the window' said Sandy Wee.

The background to the elephant trainers relationship revealed more however. For six years Said Ali, a Mahomedan, had been a very popular attraction at the zoo, particularly with young children for whom his charges performed many tricks. For health reasons, he returned to India every winter, returning for the June-to-September season. After a couple of years, Sandy Wee, a member of a Burmese religious Sect, came over in charge of a sacred white elephant, Pa Wa. He decided to remain and the zoo was happy to employ him while Said Ali was away.

Problem was, not only was Said Ali paid £2.10s a week, while Sandy Wee received only £2, but during the summer months Said Ali was again in charge of the elephants, which gave him opportunities to earn many tips, whilst Sandy Wee was sent to the sanatorium to look after the baby elephants, received no tips, and became very jealous. In addition, Said Ali did not like Sandy's religious music which also caused friction.

He was charged with the murder of Said Ali and found Guilty but the Home Secretary respited the sentence of death commuting it to penal servitude for life.[6]

NOTES FOR CHAPTER ELEVEN

1. *Whodunnit*, p30-32
2. *The Golden Age of Murder,* p118
3. *Horwell of the Yard,* p29 – 36.
4. *Police Journal*, April, 1990, p105.
5. *Ibid,* p105-123; *The Times, 4-10 March, 1930; Murder Squad* (1981), p82-94
6. *Hambrook of the Yard*, p159-165.

12

Out with the Old

In 1929 another woman joined the ranks of promising Golden Age writers when Margery Allingham's, *The Crime at Black Dudley,* was published. In this, she introduced Albert Campion, who was to become her lead character. He was another upper-class sleuth, although in this book he had only a minor role and a not too impressive one at that.

Of course it may seem risible to imagine that aristocrats or even academics of that era (or any) would be sufficiently familiar with how the other half lives or even have enough experience of varied human nature under stress to be capable of solving a murder and understanding criminals but I suppose it is no more silly than the current novel and TV fashion of having forensic scientists do the same although they, at least, do have some pertinent skills.

Margery Allingham herself was from a well-to-do family living in an old rectory in Essex run by house servants, a cook and a gardener. Both her parents were successful writers of short stories who had also dabbled in detective fiction and they encouraged Margery to write from an early age.

She and her brother were educated at home by a succession of governesses before going to boarding schools. Margery continued on afterwards to the new Regent Street Polytechnic to study music and drama, all the while writing stories and plays. In fact, her very first novel, *BLACKERCHIEF DICK: A Tale of Mersea Island*, had been published by Hodder & Stoughton back in 1923 but, although admired, had not sold well.

In *The Crime at Black Dudley* we are back in country house territory Campion being one of the young house guests at Black Dudley. However, according to *The Daily Herald,* this was not 'a slick-sy detective yarn at all but rather a tumble stumble adventure story' which featured secret panels, musty passages, blood curdling hymns in the dark and the stabbing of the host, Colonel Coombe, in an ancient ritual. 'But it often thrills quite agreeably, all the same.' *The Dundee Courier* agreed, 'the reader's interest is held to the last page.'

In one respect Margery appeared to be ahead of the curve. As Julian Symons points out in *Bloody Murder*: 'Before the end of the Twenties a certain weariness with mechanical ingenuity was beginning to be apparent and, in 1930, Anthony Berkeley noted that the old crime novel 'without the added attractions of character, style and even humour' was on its way out.

Agatha Christie had also been diversifying here and there. In *The Man in the Brown Suit* (1924) the wilful young Annie Beddingfield embarks on a helter-skelter adventure in pursuit of a murderer, having given up on the skills of the useless and quite thick Scotland Yard detective, Inspector Meadows. In the process, she also finds love. Significantly, the book was originally known as *Mystery of Mill House* and also *Anna the Adventuress*.

Then, for *Partners in Crime* (1928), two characters from Christie's second book, *The Secret Adversary*, take over a detective agency. The cases handled by Tuppence and Thomas

Beddingfield are, in fact, a collection of short stories in which the two characters act out in the style of various other Golden Age Detectives but, this Scotland Yard detective, Inspector Marriott, with whom they are collaborating, happens to be very smart.

In his fifth book Freeman Wills Crofts had also produced a police sleuth whom Martin Edwards dubbed 'the painstaking and utterly relentless Inspector Joseph French'[1] and whom Julian Symons found plodding and, since the writer had not thought it important that he should learn the details of police procedure, he had succeeded so well in making his detective commonplace (in fact, police detectives are markedly colourful characters) that he became uninteresting.[2]

In 1929, one Scotland Yard man graduated from being a pathetic also-ran to some aristocratic sleuth to actually starring in the latest thing – TALKIES – with *Behind That Curtain* from Fox Studios. True, the police detective turns out to be titled anyway and the plot has him pursue a criminal from London to India, from India to the Persian Desert and thence to San Francisco.

The Times reviewer conceded that camels and heaps of sand and an aeroplane had heightened the interest in this pursuit. 'but they do not disguise the structural weakness of the story'. The film did, however, feature Boris Karloff as a manservant and there were brief appearances of American Korean actor E L Park as Honolulu Police Inspector Charlie Chan – that detective's first outing in what were to become many from American author Earl Derr Biggers.

There was rather more approval for another crime film release, *The Crimson Circle,* which was based on an Edgar

Wallace novel in which Scotland Yard pursues the head of an international gang of murderers and blackmailers. Of course, Wallace was not a *new* crime novelist having begun writing back in 1905 with *Four Just Men*. *The Crimson Circle* had already been released as a silent film in 1922 but, in 1929, it was subject to 'a sound experiment' in which specially composed music interpreted the action and emotions of the characters. On the whole the music was 'dramatically helpful', commented *The Times*, although sometimes 'it says too much'.

There was current crime interest in the theatre too. In November, 1929, *The Times* reported that the Embassy Theatre's audience had delighted in the play, *The Edge of Life* by V Gareth Gundry, 'in which there was *no* amateur detective and in which Kerr, the professional man from Scotland Yard, was clearly heading for a nervous breakdown.'

However, Kerr Lane was *not* a detective but the Met Commissioner! Apparently, due to his 'too frequent attack on the whisky bottle' he was faced with official disgrace which was only avoided when he was shot dead in his own office – then it turned into a murder mystery. (*The Daily Telegraph* tells us that the programme was silent on Kerr's *official* police rank but *The Stage* seemed to know better.)

Another Fox film from the U.S., as I mentioned earlier, rather oddly has just the blunt title *SCOTLAND YARD*, even though it seems to have more to do with a criminal, Dakin Barrolles. After the war, Barrolles masquerades as the missing Sir John Lasher – with Lasher's wife – and is able to do this because when he was badly wounded in the war and the surgeons were rearranging his face they based it on the picture in the locket he had stolen from the Lashers. Lady Lasher (played by

Joan Bennett who is to become a famous movie star) is rather happy with this *new* version of her man. However, two other characters, who are actually German spies, threaten to tell the police – just so they can take the gold he has stolen. Barolles confesses to Inspector Cork who catches the spies and tells him he is pardoned due to his distinguished service to his country[3]. Make what you will of all that.

Meanwhile, in January, 1929, the real police saw the retirement of one of the Big Five: Albert Hawkins. He was followed out in July by Frederick Porter Wensley who, after forty-two years' service, did not regret a single day.[4]

Alas, Bouncing Albert Hawkins did not live long after his retirement. He died, aged 59, in August, 1929. His death was not unexpected, declared *The Times*, under their sub heading AN ABLE DETECTIVE, as his health had been failing when he retired in January.[5]

The cull of the first Big Five was not yet over. A year later came the following newspaper headlines:[6]

'Famous sleuth dead'

'Death of Famous Detective'

'Famous Scotland Yard Chief Dead'

The Time's report, listed in the obituaries, was headed more soberly: 'MR F CARLIN'.

The dapper, immaculate, quick-thinking and speaking 'Cocky Carlin' had, like Hawkins, also only been 59 years-old when he died.

In his recent autobiography he had supplied details of his more important cases but, oddly, had omitted one particular subject which *The Times* now focussed on:

Superintendent Carlin joined the force in 1890, his first service being in Limehouse. This was at a time when the growth of the Chinese Colony gave great anxiety to the authorities, for quite apart from the prevalence of opium there was the problem of the association of white girls with the Chinese.

The close contact he then experienced with the traffic of dangerous drugs proved most useful in after years. At the time when the traffic was at its height he was divisional detective inspector at Vine Street. The campaign of which he had control resulted in the arrest and exportation of Brilliant Chang, a young Chinese who was the central figure of a gang living luxuriously on the proceeds of selling cocaine to young men and women in whom they inculcated the habit. It was the discoveries made during these investigations that led to the framing of regulations enabling judges and magistrates to impose sentences of penal servitude on drug traffickers.[7]

'Drooper Neil' the fifth member of that first Big Five, had retired in 1927, his *Forty Years of Man-Hunting* being published in 1932 and he died in 1939 aged 72. Wensley lived on until 1949, aged 84.

In his *Detective Days,* published in 1931, Wensley explained that what had changed the *most* since his early days was that *now* the police did not suffer anywhere near the amount of violence they once had to endure. The old-time, ignorant brutal criminal had practically ceased to exist.

During his first year of service, he noted, there had been more than two thousand assaults on police and no officer could be certain whether he could pass a day without being violently attacked. And not only by criminals.

When he first went to Whitechapel there were men who made a practice of feigning to be in a drunken sleep on a doorstep but the moment a constable made an effort to rouse them they would be at his throat.

To some, he pointed out, the police were the common enemy, and it was the exception for any person to submit to arrest without putting up some sort of fight. Since that time, professional criminals had learned that violence led to heavier sentences and also not to carry burglarious tools with them lest they be stopped and searched. Now, they relied on what they could find on the spot.

There had also been a big changes due to the growth of London and the development of its' transport facilities. Criminals were no longer just crowded into certain areas such as Whitechapel. Indeed, Whitechapel was now a comparatively quiet and harmless district.

The law, too, had been brutal then with long sentences of penal servitude being handed out for relatively minor offences. He appreciated that many men became criminals through lack of opportunity or being born into that life and once a criminal it was difficult for them to change. Women, he found, seldom became master minds in crime, also due to lack of opportunity – in a different sense – although he had clearly been impressed by Mrs Bertha Weiner, the leader of a gang of German burglars, who had 'a real genius for generalship'[8].

When it came to solving crimes the most important development had of course been fingerprints. Before then, identification had been very difficult. The other major development was the one *he* had suggested and which had resulted in the formation of the famous Big Five.

Previously, as already noted, each division had its own Divisional Detective Inspector but there had been little co-operation between division or sharing of information. In 1916, when asked how to put the detective system into a more fluid state, Wensley had suggested putting senior officers in charge of supervising and co-ordinating the work of several divisions at once. But it had been wartime and the idea had been shelved until 1920 when they were on the crest of the post-war crime wave. Subsequently, the Met was divided into four with a detective Superintendent in charge of each section. They became The Big Four and when Wensley was put in control of the Central Office, they morphed into The Big Five. Having been in charge of detectives for some time Wensley was well placed to notice how varied detectives were in their skills and attitudes. For example, some were extremely clever in obtaining swift and reliable information but knew that they made bad witnesses in court so were seldom seen in the witness box. Others, were particularly good at shadowing and so forth.

As for their *personal preferences* there were those who were reluctant to associate too closely with professional criminals but preferred what he called the better class, the showier side of detective work. This was frauds and similar things. He admitted that *their* path was doubtless easier because they would be dealing mostly with members of the public rather than savvy criminals.

Much space in Wensley's book was naturally given to his earlier cases and high-profile matters such as the notorious Siege of Sidney Street. Those cases from when he was in total control were mostly seen from an over-seers point of view and of course he was, in a way, stealing some of their best stories being able to get into print ahead of them.

But he had some memorable snippets of his own, amongst them the man accused of murder but stubbornly protesting his innocence who asked, 'Tell me, Mr Wensley, if a man was to hit a woman with a hammer, not intending to kill her, and she died, would *that* be murder?'

Unsurprisingly some of his comments alluded to the fictional detectives. Pointing out that there had been all kinds of successful detectives, but they hadn't got anywhere near the top by making flashing deductions from the scratches on a watch and enmeshing a criminal by the exercise of pure reason . . .Not *one* fact, but *many*, went to prove the guilt of a criminal.

Referring to his own early learning by experience Wensley writes, 'Do not misunderstand me. I could not then, and cannot now, miraculously deduce the author of a crime from a piece of burnt matchstick.' But he could at least say, often with reasonably certainty, who was the probable author of a crime by the circumstances in which it was carried out.[9]

In other words, by local knowledge and experience. He was rather hoist by his own petard when he acknowledged that it was a matchstick stained with blood which was the first evidence which linked Robinson, the Charing Cross Trunk Murderer, with his crime.

Despite Wensley's assurance that life was now less dangerous for police officers they were, of course, still at risk. Indeed, on 24 July, 1929, as Wensley was preparing to leave, Inspector Edward Ockey of the Flying Squad was lying unconscious in the road at Kennington having been struck on the head with an iron bar after jumping on to the running board of a fleeing motor bandit's car. On 23 August, 1929, Police Constable John Self was found dying by the side of the road in Golders Green. People who went to help him heard him murmur, 'Stop him! Stop him!' He died two hours later without regaining consciousness. The cause of death was a fracture to the base of the skull.

Superintendent Cornish led the latter investigation and soon learned that a man had been seen running away from the spot and it was believed that P C Self, who was on plain clothes duty, had stopped and questioned him.

In his haste the suspect had dropped a bundle 'which' said *The Times,*' was now in possession of Scotland Yard, and may provide a valuable clue.' They also revealed that in order to acquire realistic photographs the police had used a dummy male figure placed in the exact spot where P C Self had lain.

The bundle proved to contain a black motor rug containing an old primus stove, which proved to have been stolen from a parked motor car, and also a blue rexine shopping bag with the name Mrs Holman on an attached label. The hunt for the suspect ended after four days when a man named Harry Holman handed himself in at a police station and by the time he was taken to court it had become obvious that he was simple-minded and he was remanded for a medical report.

His story was that he had been on a bus when Self had noticed the parcel and had asked whether it was his, which he denied, but nonetheless picked it up as instructed when they alighted.

At the Old Bailey Holman pleaded Not Guilty to the charge of Manslaughter while not denying that he struck Self a blow to the face with his fist (which had been witnessed) that caused the police officer to fall. He had done it, he claimed, because the parcel was *not* his, he was frightened and didn't know that

Self was a police officer and when the man had given him a push and said, 'Come on.' He became angry and struck out. He hadn't meant to kill anyone. Of course all this was from *his* point of view, Self being dead.

It was revealed that Holman had spent time in mental homes and that he had been registered as feeble-minded. The jury found him Guilty but made a strong recommendation to mercy – which he certainly received with a sentence of only eight months. The question of the shopping bag carrying Mrs Holman's name being in the bundle with stolen property was not addressed. Perhaps her husband was not so simple after all?

The motor bandits who felled Inspector Ockey were arrested at the time when one of their tires burst as they sped away. The Inspector recovered after two months. One of the bandits received four years and the other five years penal servitude for grievous bodily harm on Ockey and assault on another officer as well as for going equipped with house-breaking implements.

As Wensley was leaving big changes were taking place at Scotland Yard. The C.I.D. was to be increased by fifty officers. Bringing their strength up to 980. According to *The Times* this was partly to cope with the increase in motor bandit gangs.

Superintendent Ashley replaced Wensley as Chief and the other members of the Big Five were to be Superintendent Cooper to head the Western Division 'where his experience in raiding night clubs and enquiring into the ramifications of the activities of undesirable aliens will be of utmost service'; Superintendent Cornish 'who has a well-deserved reputation for dealing with serious crime' and being largely responsible for bringing Robinson the trunk murderer to justice as well as having 'many other clever captures to his credit' would take over the Northern area; Superintendent Savage, currently at Central Office, would take over the Eastern area and Superintendent Brown was already in control of the Southern area 'where the Croydon arsenic poisoner has kept him busy for some months'.[10]

To Superintendent Nichols would go the responsibility for the Central Office 'from where detectives are sent, at short notice, to deal with murder cases in any part of the country where their help is desired, as well as to track down 'crooks' of every type who betray their presence in London.'

Divisional Detective Inspector Helby was promoted to Chief Inspector at Scotland Yard while Chief Inspector Hambrook would get charge of the Flying Squad again.[11]

Meanwhile, the motor bandits were running riot in London. On one occasion they made a large haul in a smash and grab raid of a jeweller's shop in Bond Street then drove out of the city in the direction of Bath. However, a police constable alerted the new Reading Flying Squad who pursued the car on motor cycles and motor cars until the bandits turned around and headed straight back to London. The Reading Squad kept up the pursuit for 15 miles but lost sight of them near Maidenhead.

Things hotted up towards Christmas with more smash and grab raids and two new phenomena. Firstly, handbag snatching from motor cars. A smartly-dressed man would step out of the car in a well-to-do district, apparently to ask his way, then carry out the snatch. There had been two dozen such offences in a few weeks in the Dulwich district, reported *The Times* on 23 December.

However, the strangest and most epidemic phenomena at the time was the slashing of plate glass windows. Things had improved, reported *The Times,* on Friday, 20 September,

1929, under the heading SLASHING OF SHOP WINDOWS. Yesterday only 300 windows had been affected whilst the previous day there had been 600. They occurred all over London although Merton and Wimbledon were the worst.

There was 'a further outbreak in Leicester' on Wednesday and there had been cases in Exeter, Stamford and Derby. Much of the damage was only minor but there was no explanation for this habit although, in one case, the arresting officer had asked for a remand for medical reports because he didn't think the offender was responsible for his actions and another was for a jewellery raid.

NOTES FOR CHAPTER TWELVE

1. The Golden Age of Murder, p75

2. Bloody Murder, p114

3. Wikipedia: *Scotland Yard* (1930 film)

4. Detective Days, p288

5. The Times, 20 August, 1929

6. Lincolnshire Echo, 27 September, 1930; *Sheffield Independent,* 29 September, 1930; *The Northern Daily Mail,* 27 September, 1930

7. The Times, 29 September, 1930

8. Detective Days, p40

9. Ibid, p17 *and* p67-8

10. See Note 16 after the following chapter.[11]

11. The Times, 2 August, 1929; 5 August, 1929 and 6 August, 1929

13

A very theatrical affair

Scotland Yard detectives *en route* to assist another force usually had *some* idea what kind of world they were about to enter. It might be a historic small city with a tiny police force; a large county force in a rural farming area or a grimy industrial metropolis, each having its own history, habits, dialects and prejudices.

However, even the confident and experienced team of Chief Inspector Berrett and Sergeant Harris who, in June 1929, were instructed to 'proceed forthwith' to 'render assistance' to the Reading police regarding a robbery with violence in that prosperous railway town some 38 miles West of London, could scarcely have expected that they were about to become so immersed in the world of theatre.

The victim, Mr Alfred Oliver, had been attacked in his tobacconist shop in Cross Street in the town centre and was taken to hospital suffering from severe head wounds. Money was missing from his till. On Berrett's arrival at the scene he was greeted by Mrs Oliver who told him that her husband had just died. It was now a murder and lone shopkeeper murders, like those of prostitutes, were particularly difficult to solve due to the plethora of possible suspects who may have no personal connection with the victim.

Berrett must have gritted his teeth when local Detective Sergeant Pope informed him that he had cleaned all the blood from the shop floor and removed the broken arm of the shop scales; Mr Oliver's splintered spectacles; and his shattered false teeth. But D S Pope had, at least, had the sense to carefully note where all these things *had* been and, thank goodness, had not cleaned away what appeared to be a bloodstained thumb print on the glass of a show case. Berrett phoned the Yard requesting a fingerprints expert and a photographer.

Many possible suspects had been spotted near the shop and its entrance at the pertinent time. The most promising by a Mrs Jackson who had bumped into a man just outside the shop but she had refused to give a written statement to the local police. Despite the late hour. It was 10.15pm – Berrett insisted on seeing her immediately. But she refused to have anything put in writing until her husband agreed. She would do so the following morning.

The following evening she was still refusing to commit herself and was altering the original time of her sighting. Berrett, usually a kind and patient man with charming manners, lost patience with her, forming the opinion that she was 'a gossiping type of woman' whose evidence would be of little use anyway and gave her a sharp little lecture and some advice on her civic duty[1]. Since he was a very large and prepossessing man this would have given most people pause.

However, there was a sudden light at the end of the tunnel with the news that a man in nearby Pangbourne village had given himself up to police as the murderer. Berrett and Harris hurried there only to find a 61-year-old tailor of no fixed abode who had clearly been drinking and who told a rambling and inaccurate tale which, they quickly realised, was a bogus confession.[2]

The inquest on Mr Oliver, which opened the following afternoon, was particularly noteworthy due to the hospital doctor's description of Mr Oliver's horrific injuries. He had nineteen lacerations to his scalp; three large depressed fractures of the vault; a fracture across the base of the skull and fractures to both the upper and lower jaw. All caused by a very heavy instrument. Clearly the attack had been ferocious. There followed several suggestions as to what 'the instrument' might have been but none were conclusive. Then, to give police time to investigate, the proceedings were adjourned *sine die.*

Meanwhile, Berrett received the news that a 21-year-old by the name of George Charles Jeffries had been in Mr Oliver's shop at about the time the attack was thought to have taken place. He pulled him in for questioning and received the extraordinary news that Jeffries had indeed been in the shop – to buy a packet of Players cigarettes. That no-one had come to serve him so he had knocked on the counter. Then, hearing a tapping sound coming from behind it, leaned over and saw a man's legs. He had become frightened and ran out, briefly returned to his place of work, then home, without telling anyone or fetching help. His excuse was that he had just been to see his sister who was dying of tuberculosis and he had been confused and frightened. And, indeed, his sister did die – that night.[3]

Complicating issues came with various other sightings and fragments of information which Berrett and Harris winnowed out: Mr Oliver had recently been worried about the possibility of a burglary and had given instructions that the passenger door to the rear be kept closed at all times then there was the suspicious movements of a man in a blue suit and a man in a dark suit seen in the street outside the shop – with variations to their descriptions and movements.

A butcher, Mr Loxton, thought blue-suit man was about five foot eight with a full face, hatless, and with long hair 'in a rough state'. A Mrs Shepherd claimed to have seen a man of about 25 to 26 years old, about five foot seven, of stocky build, who had run out of the shop at about eight minutes past six and run down the street.

The man in the dark suit had been seen acting very strangely – talking to himself, bumping into people, wearing a raincoat thrown over his shoulders in a cape fashion and had probably been drinking. But the most vital sighting was a report from a Mrs Alice James who had seen a hatless man with blood on his face standing in the doorway of Mr Oliver's shop.[4]

Then came the information from Twickenham in London that police were holding a man named Miles who claimed to know two criminal brothers who had committed the crime. Harris brought him to Reading. But the men he had accused, though criminal, turned out to have no convictions for violence – Miles himself proved had been a patient in a mental hospital.[5] . . . And so it went on. All playing out in the newspapers, including, at last, Mrs Jackson's story now titled 'The Man with the Staring Eyes'.

Alas, there was no forensic evidence: the weapon had not been found and the smudged thumbprint turned out to belong to George Taylor, a friend who had been called to the scene by the distressed wife.

The water was further muddied by the presence of many strangers due to the races being held in nearby Ascot and Windsor and this day being known as Black Saturday for the number of dubious strangers there would be in town.

A tramp in Winchester told the police that on June 22nd he had seen a man throw what looked like a bloodstained parcel over a railway bridge near Reading. It was arranged for him to come along the following morning. Berrett had the line and the trains searched but no parcel was found.

More possible leads were followed up and, later, a man, in faraway Glasgow, confessed to having committed the murder with two accomplices. He appeared quite sane and his story was convincing enough for Glasgow police to charge him with the murder. Berrett had him brought to Reading where he duly repudiated all he had previously confessed to explaining that he suffered from 'confusional psychosis' and had heard voices accusing him of the murder. He had not been the same since being buried by a shell burst on the Somme.[6] Meanwhile, a man named Joseph Cassidy was walking into Blackheath Police Station admitting to the murder. He, too, proved delusional.[7]

It was all looking pretty desperate when, suddenly, what appeared to be a *real* breakthrough occurred when Reading's Chief Constable, Thomas Alfred Burrows, was approached by a member of the public who told him, 'That chap you're looking for with the frizzy hair is Yale Drew, that actor in *The Monster*.'

He was referring to the man reputed to have been seen by Mrs James with blood on his face standing in the doorway of Mr Oliver's shop. Philip Yale Drew was an American who had achieved fame in cowboy movies before being coaxed across the Atlantic by the famous actress Ellen Terry. He had gone on to star in London's West End although, more recently, had dropped down the acting ladder onto the less glamorous British provincial theatre touring circuit and had, at the time of the murder, been appearing in a play called *The Monster* at Reading's County Theatre.

It was quickly established that Drew was still with the touring company who were currently appearing in St Helen's, Lancashire, and were due, the coming week, at the Palace Theatre in Nottingham. Chief Constable Burrrows and Sergeant Harris drove there to meet him. It was now a month since the murder had occurred.

They found Drew partially dressed having his breakfast in his lodgings. Unsurprisingly, he was startled when requested to come to the police station to be interviewed about the murder but it was his hysterical manageress, Margaret Lindo, who was to give Harris his first taste of theatrics with, 'Oh, Philip, what have you done now!' and swaying as she exclaimed, 'Hold me – I'm going to faint!'

She recovered and it was her husband Frank who continued the performance with a booming, 'Oh, this is *ridiculous!*' accompanied by appropriately raised eyebrows and spread hands.[8]

At the station Drew was told he resembled the bloodied man seen in the doorway and questioned for three hours. Later, he informed *The Nottingham Evening Post* that, being an actor, he was always seeking new experiences and had spent most of his time in Reading walking about and visiting shops so it was quite possible he had gone into the shop of the unfortunate man who was murdered for a packet of cigarettes. If so, he did not recall it.

All of which admission, Berrett noted, was the opposite of what he had said in his statement to them.

After one performance, Frank Lindo addressed the audience (possibly hoping to profit from the exposure) telling them that one of their company had been accused of being an accomplice in a murder and adding, 'We who *know* him realise that such a charge is absolutely futile and absurd.' Drew himself was called forth and bowed to the audience but his emotions overwhelmed him and he broke down.[9]

Sergeant Harris interviewed him again. This time he became very excited, refusing to sign the caution, saying that he was an American subject and they were interfering with his liberty. Then he began to cry.[10]

Meanwhile, in the background, there was much activity as police followed him and attempted to locate and collect all of his clothes which he seemed to have made strenuous efforts either to clean himself or take to a cleaners. But their attempts to reveal that they had been originally bloodstained failed. However, there *was* the parcel he was thought to have taken with him when he left Reading.

They interviewed him again when he reached St Albans and *this* time he gave details of 'his horrible ordeal' to the National Press, including the *Daily Mail* and *The Daily Herald*.

By now, Berrett had had twelve reported sightings of the man said to look like Drew acting strangely and confused and the 'plump and homely' Mrs James had identified Drew as the man with blood on his face. In fact, the actor was an alcoholic and he quite often behaved strangely. Berrett also knew that Drew had enquired at two other tobacconists that day about the decorative smokers pipes they were displaying. (He was in the habit of occasionally sending such items to a favourite relative and friend back home.) On this occasion the pipes were too expensive. His funds were low.

Reading had not seen a murder since 1895 and this one, featuring a famous film actor, was attracting such countrywide attention particularly via Drew's interviews with the Press. By the 8th of October, the sixth day of the reconvened inquest, the excitement was becoming intense. Although the latest inquest sitting was not due to begin until 2 p.m., by 8 a.m. many members of the public (mostly female) had begun to queue outside the court, bringing with them camp stools and their lunch. A downpour at 11 a.m. did not deter them – they had also brought their umbrellas and macs. By 1.30 p.m. hundreds of people lined the streets to cheer the actor *en route* from his hotel to the courtroom.

The second witness to give evidence that afternoon was 'woman shopper', Mrs Florence Wheeler, who reported that, at the time in question, she had almost bumped into a man walking very quickly away from Cross Street. He had been wearing his coat slung over his shoulders 'like a cloak' – an actorly thing to do. She had also seen him there on the previous day 'from my bedroom window' – coat worn in the same manner. She thought the man looked something like the man now pointed out to her as Mr Yale Drew.

The next witness was Scotland Yard's Detective Sergeant Harris. Like Berrett a substantial and confident figure. He described how on 7 August he had gone to St Albans Police Station to question Drew further and to pick up a pair of the actor's blue trousers which had been missing but had just mysteriously reappeared with a cleaning ticket attached.

Police had not yet traced the cleaners. The Coroner appealed to the Press to help identify them and sought assurance from D S Harris that the actor had been sober when he made his statement and not under any duress.

The sergeant was asked about an article in a Sunday paper headed WHAT I TOLD POLICE AFTER THE SHOP CRIME which was 'purported to be written by Mr Drew'. (In it, he had claimed that the police had asked him about his statement that he had carried some liver home in his pocket in which he had said 'Some blood from the liver may have got into the pocket'.)

Sergeant Harris responded bluntly, 'That question was never asked.'

'A scientific explanation. Possibly well thought out,' commented the Coroner.

However, by now Mr Drew had acquired a leading defence lawyer, Mr Fearnley-Whittingstall and, reported *The Times*, there were several sharp passages between him and Sergeant Harris – mostly concerning the colour of Mr Drew's hair.

'You said yesterday that Mr Drew's hair had changed?'

'Yes.'

'Are you suggesting that Mr Drew is dying his hair?'

'I am.'

Had he any evidence, any suggestion, any date on which to make that statement?

'My own eyes.'

'You mean', enquired Counsel, 'your own guesswork?'

'Certainly not. Why, it is apparent to everybody in court. It is my job to notice things like that. I have noticed something about yourself, for instance. The handkerchief in your pocket now has a red laundry mark (laughter) I only mention that because it is my job to notice these things.'

The extraordinary exchange went on. Despite the eminence of the detective's art, continued the Counsel, Mr Drew was prepared to let any chemist in the country examine his hair to prove that it had not been dyed.

' I give evidence of what I see,' countered Harris.

Right, *when* had he dyed it?

'Since I saw him on 7 August his hair has changed colour. Then it was brown; now it is not brown.'

Clearly, Harris was suggesting that Drew was trying to disguise himself.

'Could he,' asked Fearnley-Whittingstall, 'out of fairness to Mr Drew, on behalf of the police, take the step to prove whether he was right or wrong?'

'It does not lie with me.'

Counsel changed tack – had Mr Drew not given him all the help he could and answered all his questions?'

'Certainly.'

'He has helped you all he could?'

Harris was not going to fall for that and answered, ' I do not say he has helped us all he could.' (He had not, for instance, confessed.)

The jury foreman began questioning the sergeant about hair dyes but he pointed out that he was *not* a hairdresser. The foreman assured the court that *he* had certainly noticed that the actor's hair was greyer than it had been and that the jury had also noticed that it had changed colour whilst he had been in court during the last few days.[11]

Sergeant Harris's attitude may have been influenced by the fact that when questioning Drew at Nottingham and St Albans he had been obliged to endure some more actorly histrionics and found some of the man's replies evasive. Then there was his constant grandstanding with the Press, denial of all possible adverse evidence and a useful forgetfulness. But it certainly appeared that the Coroner had encouraged this attitude towards the actor by peremptorily ordering him to stand up to be identified and making pointed comments.

Further witnesses recalled seeing a man *like* Drew in the area of the tobacconists that day and several times Drew was ordered by the Coroner to stand up to see whether he was that man.

When the actor himself gave evidence he denied leaving on his make-up and false beard on the night after the murder as one of the witnesses had accused him of doing but admitted that he *may* have removed it carelessly which could have prompted the witness and his own landlady to suggest otherwise.

The following day came the Coroner's summing up and it didn't exactly *clear* Drew – rather reiterated the sighting of a man *like* him being in the area, four witnesses positively identifying the man as Drew and one saying that he resembled the man he had seen.

As they awaited the jury's verdict the crowds gathering in and around the court, jamming the street outside from one end to the other, grew more fevered. The jury took their time but, eventually, it came: 'wilful murder by some person or persons unknown'. The crowd went wild. The actor was treated like a conquering hero ending up thanking 'the best audience of my life' from the balcony of The Great Western Hotel. He was in heaven. Sure that he had been cleared of all suspicion and certain that he could now resume his life and career.

Alas, it didn't work out like that.

From then on Philip Yale Drew, once a star in cowboy films and on the West End stage, found it impossible to get work. Too many doubts had been sown. He had been too equivocal and evasive about his movements. He had kept on saying that he couldn't remember. Which could have been true if he was drunk at the time.

So, was he guilty or not? Well-known crime writer, Richard Whittington-Egan, was so moved by the man's subsequent plight that he set out to do an extremely thorough investigation of his life and the case which had brought him down – even travelling to the United States to interview his family and friends.

His book, *The Ordeal of Philip Yale Drew*, published in 1972, 38 years after the murder, and 28 years after the death of Philip Yale Drew, was pretty clearly on Drew's side. So many friends and acquaintances had spoken about the man's kindness and insisted that he could not possibly have committed murder. But the author did uncover evidence that Drew could be violent. One old friend, actor manager Andrew Melville, thought Drew 'just a big cuddly bear of a man and a very sweet person' but admitted that he had seen him violent. 'One night – he was drunk of course – he went for his dresser over some trifling thing he had done or omitted to do, and nearly throttled him.'[12]

Whittington-Egan also interviewed Sergeant Harris 'still an immense, rumbling giant of a man, unbowed, clear of mind and eye'. He was in no doubt that Drew had committed the murder, as were Berrett and the local police sergeant. They felt he had done it in a drunken frenzy, was now sorry about it and they wouldn't have liked to see him hang.

A member of the Coroner's jury told the author that they *had* been about to *name* Drew as the murderer but two members resisted because they wanted to get home and were frightened of the crowd's reaction should they do so. So much for justice.

Dolores, a woman with whom Drew had been briefly associated since the case, had asked to see Sergeant Harris as she lay dying and told him that Drew had confessed his guilt to her. They were quarrelling while he was drunk and he had tried to throttle her exclaiming, 'I've done one murder and I'll do another.'[13] Whittington-Egan felt this 'confession' may have been just to frighten her.

In answer to another mystery – why the inhabitants of Reading has so supported him – the widow of his counsel, Fearnley-Whittingstall, felt they saw the man being bullied, railroaded by the coroner and police and didn't like it (although she told him that her husband had *not* felt the police were out to get Drew.)[14]

His treatment by the Coroner did arouse some public disquiet and there were questions asked of the Home Secretary in Parliament as to whether he would consider forming a committee to look at and clarify the powers of coroners. But it came to nothing. The murder remained unsolved and, on New Year's Day, 1930, a report in the *Taunton Courier* and *Western Advertiser* and many other newspapers offered an explanation headed:

UNSOLVED MURDERS
ONE OF SCOTLAND YARD'S WORST YEARS
DETECTIVE HANDICAP

To prove their point they listed the Reading Shop Murder,

The Croydon Poisonings, the Camberwell Singing Rosie Murder and the Eltham Train Murder – although it assured its readers that in the latter case the detectives had 'very clear ideas'.

They revealed that among criminologists this black period was thought to be due largely to the recent Royal Commission on Police Procedures which had severely handicapped the police. A detective explained that they were 'now compelled to exercise a degree of caution that is almost absurd. The suspected person enjoys far more privileges than honest taxpaying customers.' For example, police were unable to ask a suspect about any implement which he might have borrowed and which could implicate him.

The Commission which Police historian, David Ascoli, described as 'An example of a sledge hammer to crack a nut and of the use of the triumph of prejudice over reason'[15] had come about largely as a reaction to the Savidge Case.[16]

THE CROYDON POISONINGS: Alleged mismanaged Coroners' enquiries also featured in this case in which, between April, 1928 and March, 1929, three members of the same family died of arsenic poisoning; 59-year-old colonial civil servant Edmund Creighton Duff; his sister-in-law Vera Sydney and Violet Duff a 49-year-old single woman.

All their exhumed bodies contained arsenic but the Coroner had failed to take the advice of the Director of Public Prosecutions and held each inquest separately which led to confusion and even to some specimens becoming mixed up. Much suspicion centered around Grace Duff, widow of Edmund, but there was insufficient evidence to bring a charge. In his book, *The Mystery of Birdhurst Drive: The Croydon*

Poisonings, Richard Whittington-Egan decides that Grace was indeed the culprit the motive being her love affair with a local doctor and hatred of her husband. The other two murders, of Vera and Violet, were for gain.

THE ELTHAM TRAIN MURDER took place on 13 March, 1929, no-one was sure how. Twenty-eight-year-old Mrs Winifred Maud East was found decapitated on the railway line between Kidbrooke and Eltham. It was known that the carriage which she had entered at Barnehurst in South West London had been empty at the time but as the train started a young man was seen to jump in.

Between Kidbrooke and Eltham screams were heard, apparently coming from the carriage, and the following day her body was found on the line. The Coroner thought the principal question was how had she got out of the door? Was it deliberate because she was terrified – or had she been pushed? Either way it was murder and the jury agreed – by some person or persons unknown.

THE CAMBERWELL SINGING ROSIE MURDER: a similar verdict was given on the death of 45-year-old married women, Mrs Katherine Peck who was known as Singing Rosie, who had been found in a roadway near her home with her throat cut. Although, in this case, 43-year-old Frederick George Murphy, a ship's fireman, was charged with her murder but he was acquitted at the Old Bailey.

He was known to keep her company and he had confessed to a friend when he had got back to his lodging house that he was minus his overcoat and other clothes likely to be bloodstained but the jury were instructed that it would be unwise to convict. However, he *was* convicted of murder – eight years later – but of a different woman (Mrs Rosina Field) who had been found strangled in the cellar of a furniture shop in Islington in which Murphy had been employed as an odd job man. As with the first murder, he had come forward to give himself up declaring he had merely found Rosina's body and had hidden it for fear that police would not believe him. He was right. He was found Guilty and hanged but did not go quietly – shouting and protesting all the way about that much being made in the Press that it was his repeat offence.[17]

NOTES FOR CHAPTER THIRTEEN

1. *The Ordeal of Philip Yale Drew*, p37-8 and 41; *Western Daily Press*, 25 June, 1929.

2. *Ibid*, p41-42

3. Ibid, p47-48; *The Times,* 3 July, 1929

4. *Ibid*, p53; *Dundee Evening Telegraph*, 3 October, 1929?

5. *Ibid*, p55

6. *Ibid*, p251-254; *The Times,* 30 October, 1929

7. *Ibid*, 254

8. *The Times,* 9 October, 1929; *Midland Daily Telegraph*, 9 October, 1929; *Derby Daily Telegraph,* 9 October, 1929

9. *The Ordeal of Philip Yale Drew*, p67-68; *Nottingham Journal*, 15 October, 1929.

10. *The Times, 9 October, 1929 and Ibid, p68*

11. Ibid & *The Ordeal of Philip Yale Drew,* p172-181

12. *Ibid,* p330

13. *Ibid,* p336

14. *Ibid,* p338

15. *The Queen's Peace*, p214

16. See Note 1, Chapter 15

17. The Evening Telegraph & The Liverpool Echo, 17 August, 1937.

14

New Blood and Fewer Puzzles

The close of the 1920s was also the end of the first ten years of the Golden Age of detective stories. Of course, the genre had been developing in its own way on the other side of the Atlantic but one author was to muddy these waters somewhat at the start of the second period.

He was John Dickson Carr, son of a U.S. Congressman from Pennsylvania who was to marry an Englishwoman and come to live in the U.K. In 1929, he launched into detective novels with *It Walks By Night* in which a newlywed young man has his head chopped off in a locked room. His sleuth was Detective Bercolin of the Paris Police.

This very prolific writer was to set most of his novels in England and, indeed, his two most regular sleuths were upper class Englishmen: the egg-head Dr Gideon Fell and Sir Henry Merrivale (the latter books under the name of Carter Dickson) and the locked room mystery was to be his speciality.

In one of their advertisements his publishers printed *The Daily Telegraph's* review

'Terrifying mystery . . .a classic of crime' alongside a quote from Irish writer and crime critic St John Ervine: 'Dazzlingly thrilling.' They also gave *It Walks By Night* an attention-grabbing send off with a Press advert announcing that they had sealed the last section of the book 'and if you can stop at the seal your bookseller will refund your money'.

All this worked. By 1931 there were two more books featuring Henri Bercolin and the following year another two. Then Dr Fell and Sir Henry Merrivale took over at about the same pace.

Also introduced in 1929 was the first of the 'gentlemen cops' – Inspector John Poole -- who arrived in Henry Wade's third detective novel, *The Duke of York's Steps*. Wade, whose real name was Henry Lancelot Aubrey-Fletcher, was at a distinct advantage in the gentleman business being a member of the landed gentry himself. He was also something of an insider on police matters having served as a Justice of the Peace.

Martin Edwards finds Wade's storylines 'often strikingly original' and thinks that he reveals a keen awareness of the responsibilities that accompany the privileges of leadership within the police or anywhere else, and wonders whether it was Wade's background which had led to the excellence of his crime fiction being often overlooked.[1]

At the end of 1929 and the start of 1930 came the birth of The Detection Club, an organisation which would allow crime novelists to gather to socialise, exchange useful knowledge, complain about publishers and enjoy a good meal.

The driving force behind its birth was Anthony Berkeley who was currently enjoying great success with his *The Poisoned Chocolates Case* which Julian Symons described as 'one of the most stunning trick stories in the history of detective fiction'[2]. After Berkeley and his wife hosted convivial dinners for detective fiction writers he proposed the idea of a club and began inviting talented detective fiction authors to join. Dorothy L Sayers became an enthusiastic promoter and an eager publicity aide.

During its' first year (1930) twenty-eight authors were voted in. Out of the various proposals for communal activities which gradually arose was the idea of a Detective Annual (this was superseded by a multi-authored novel, (*The Floating Admiral*) and *Behind the Screen,* a BBC serial by six members, with a follow -up, 'Plotting a Detective Story' by Sayers and Berkeley.[3]

Having been involved in a fairly casual attempt at a multi-authored crime novel I know how difficult it can be to keep up the impetus and make the whole thing hang together as a book. Not for the Detection Club members though; the *The Floating Admiral* proved to be a triumph. According to Martin Edwards it was widely regarded as the most successful chain novel, and the most popular collaborative crime novel ever published – 'a Golden Age classic complete with a map showing the scene of the crime.' The rules (laid down by Sayers) said that each writer should have a definite solution in mind and must not add fresh complications without having any idea of how to resolve them.[4]

Not all was so encouraging. Lt.Colonel Frank Carter, the new head of Scotland Yard's Special Branch, gave crime novelists a talk in which he duly informed them that they had got the Scotland Yard man all wrong. This event was described at great length and in a rather over-written style in *The Graphic* by former war correspondent and current thriller writer Valentine Williams – the man who had inspired Wade to start writing after listening to his talk on detective fiction in France just after the Armistice.[5]

Williams now noted that Lt Colonel Carter had told them there was nowhere near *that* many murders in real life (which was something they had been told before[6]) and anyway that burglars were much more interesting, cleverer and more plucky. Williams countered that the first duty of a novelist was 'to interest' and to provide a thrill. A murder, with its blood, eyes wide with terror and a death sentence in the last chapter provided that. He did, however, concede that the character, habits and methods of most fictional detectives were 'wildly improbable'. 'Unfortunately, there are so many horribly incompetent detective stories published nowadays that it is not permissible to say that crime novels as a body recognise the truth of this expert criticism. Nonetheless, the simple fact was that an investigation as carried out by Scotland Yard was too commonplace and had too much 'rule of thumb' about it to be thrilling and, in his, experience police detectives were 'of identical type' – reserved, competent individuals running to a dusty bowler, thick boots and an umbrella.

He went on:

'There was the late Chief Inspector Mercer, for instance, who handled a somewhat sensational jewel robbery of which a member of my family was a victim. He would be well described in Col. Carter's terms as "a rather nice human being". He impressed me as being a just and kindly man, imbued, like every detective I have ever encountered, with a faintly suspicious air. He was not the least dramatic even when he detected, as he did almost instantly, the thief, for the simple reason that the thief was an "old lag" and the Inspector recognised him. For the rest, Inspector Mercer carried no magnifying glass, had no tricks, and travelled in buses.' (Another of Williams's points was that real-life detectives would never be able to live the spacious life-style of his fictional representation. 'For him the bus, the tube, the push bike and a little house in Balham in place of a high-powered motor car, the first-class sleeper . . .the chambers in Albany or on Park Avenue.'

Neither had the foreign detectives he had met impressed him. **The French – member of the Surete:** 'Quiet, round-faced little man who, in his rusty black suit and straw hat, might have been anything from a schoolteacher to a rent collector.' **American – leader of New York detectives:** Grey-haired, soft of voice and gentle of visage, he suggested an Irish country practitioner or small tradesman rather than the chief of the force marshalled against the bewilderingly large number of crimes which take place yearly in Manhattan.' The only one with 'any real dramatic flavour about him' had been **the German** but Williams didn't say in what way.

Finally, Williams declares: ' Colonel Carter may shake a kindly finger at us, the crime novelists. But we have no intention of mending our ways. The public would not let us, even if we would.'[7]

Although nominally in charge of the Flying Squad, from July, 1929, Detective Chief Inspector Hambrook was sent out of London rather frequently to deal with cases with which Scotland Yard had been called upon to assist. This may have been because the Yard was finding the calls on the Murder Squad more than they could handle and were obliged to send a Detective *Chief* Inspector if possible.

One of these cases was another shopkeeper murder which had even less hope of being solved than the Reading crime, but for different reasons. The curious case of The Ramsgate Tuckshop Murder first came to light on 20 September, 1930, when a twelve-year-old girl named Ellen Marvel was sent by her mother to buy a blancmange powder from 82-year-old Miss Margery Wren who ran the shop opposite. Ellen found the door locked but by giving it a rattle she roused Miss Wren from her chair in the back room and she opened up.

When she did, the startled girl saw blood running down the old lady's face. It took her time to get Miss Wren to understand that she wanted vanilla not raspberry flavour blancmange powder. They were interrupted by the girl's father shouting across telling her to hurry up as he wanted to go to the pictures with her mother. Ellen shouted back, 'Come and look at Miss Wren. Her face is covered in blood.'

Miss Wren gave conflicting information to the doctor and a relative who was summoned. She had fallen over the fire tongs which lay nearby. Then, to P C Arthur, 'over a poker'. Later, she described how a man had caught her by the throat and set about her with the tongs.

Alternatively, she talked about just falling over, and insisted that no-one had attacked her. Then it was two men who had done so. But it soon became obvious to the doctor that she was trying to screen somebody. 'He has escaped, Doctor,' she told him eventually, 'and you will never get him.'

Neither the vicar, nor the magistrate who took her dying declaration, could prise the information from her. 'I know I am going home,' she told him. 'I do not wish him to suffer. He must bear his sins. I do not wish to make a statement.' And she closed her eyes and died shortly afterwards.

In a sense it seemed she may have brought her fate upon

herself. Not normally a very communicative person she had dropped hints to some she knew well that she owned some property, had about £1,000 invested in Government Bonds and that she had a few pounds in tin boxes around the house although, at the same time, she pleaded poverty.

By the time Hambrook got there she was comatose and never rallied enough for him to speak to her. However, in her ramblings since acquiring her injuries she had mentioned several names and all had to be checked up on including one young man who had lied about his whereabouts *in case* he was suspected but it turned out that he was innocent, and Miss Wren went to her grave with her secret intact.[8]

In October, 1930, it was back down to *another* resort on the Kent coast for Hambrook – to the popular resort of Margate – for the case in which Sidney Henry Fox was suspected of murdering his mother so that he might benefit from her life insurance policy. They were an itinerant couple who booked into good hotels then left without paying their bills.

Sidney was no stranger to Hambrook who had arrested him thirteen years earlier at the Royal Automobile Club for forging a cheque in the name of an officer in the Royal Air Force.

At the time, Fox had been 18-years-old and, as wrote Hambrook later in his memoirs, 'was then regarded as a dangerous and unscrupulous scoundrel.'.

The case at Margate turned out to be a complex one which was to become very well known due to the fact that a Doctor Bronte and the well-known professor of forensic medicine, Sydney Smith, disagreed with the ever-confident Sir Bernard Spilsbury about his evidence. *He* claimed that Mrs Fox had been strangled before being found overcome by a fire in her room because *he* had found a bruise on her larynx – which *they* had not seen although her hyoid bone was not broken as would be expected. Spilsbury would not be moved but there was sufficient evidence against the son, including his last-minute extension of the insurance policy to make sure it would just cover the time she was scheduled to die. He was found Guilty and hanged.[9]

Since his successful handling of the Pembridge Square murder in 1928 the keen, Divisional Detective Inspector John Horwell, had been promoted to Chief Inspector and placed on the Murder Squad rota at Scotland Yard. In his book, *Horwell of the Yard,* he felt obliged to point out that for such progress hard work was necessary particularly if, like him, you were ill-educated. Indeed. he lists his progression:

June 6th, 1909, appointed to the rank of Detective Constable.

September 5th, 1913, promoted to the rank of Detective-Sergeant 3rd Class

June 24th, 1920, advanced to the rank of Detective Sergeant 2nd Class

June 5th, 1922, advanced to the rank of Detective Sergeant Ist Class

May 25th, 1925, promoted to rank of Detective Inspector 2nd Class

March 10th, 1927, promoted to rank of Acting Divisional Detective-Inspector

May 30th, 1927, promoted to rank of Divisional Detective Inspector Ist Class

April 21st, 1931, promoted to the rank of Chief Inspector, C.I.D.

Which was where he was now and, he confesses, it had not been easy.

'My worst patch was when I was preparing myself for promotion from constable to sergeant. To attain the latter rank I had to pass for a Second Class Civil Service Certificate. That came hard upon me, having had very little schooling. There was only one thing for it – I went to school again. Not day school, of course, but in the evenings in my own time. And how I sweated at those classes! I attended them for years and gradually made up for lost time. I entered my examination for promotion to sergeant with misgivings, but I am glad to state that I went through first time!'

Things were so much better now, he pointed out. There were police schools where every constable had a thorough training. Not only that, they had a break for rest and refreshment in the middle of their eight-hour shifts and a day off every week.

Horwell was first on call when, at 10pm on August Bank Holiday Monday, 1931, a request for assistance with a murder case came in from Oxford City Police. By midnight, he was on a train from Paddington.

The victim was 54-year-old widow Mrs Louisa Kempson who had been found lying on the floor of her semi-detached villa whom, as he recalled in his memoirs, had clearly been 'the victim of unbridled ferocity'. There was a wound in the centre of her forehead 'which had probably been inflicted by a hammer', another on the back of her head, and a sharp instrument had clearly been thrust through her throat. The latter, most likely, Horwell surmised, was because the murderer realised that the first two wounds had not yet caused her death which led to the possibility that the victim may have recognised her killer. Spilsbury later opined that she had still been alive when the sharp cutting instrument had been driven through her neck, severing the carotid artery.

The house had been ransacked. Mrs Kempson had been left a great deal of property by her husband so the supposition would probably have been that there was much money and many valuables secreted about the place. Three empty purses were found but one small one had been missed and it appeared that the intruder had not realised that a box supporting a crucifix was hollow and contained gold pieces. Unfortunately, there were no helpful clues or signs of the weapons but, tucked away behind a mirror, were several old visiting cards and these were all followed up and the house-to-house enquiries were extended ever outwards. Nonetheless, nine days after the estimated time of the murder there was little progress and a growing sense of desperation in the team.

Suddenly, help arrived in the form of Mrs Alice Mary Andrews who lived ten minutes away from the scene. She told a constable that a man named Seymour, from whom she had bought a vacuum cleaner two years earlier, had called on the Bank holiday Friday. He had called several times before – to check her machine was working – but not recently. This time, he gave her a hard luck story of how he had been swimming in the Thames when some youths had stolen his money, and she lent him four shillings and sixpence. He came back later that day saying he had missed his bus home and she allowed him to stay the night. Most vitally, she noticed he had a parcel with him and, examining it, she found it contained a hammer and chisel. Also, she knew that the victim had bought a vacuum cleaner from him.

Horwell must have thought all his birthdays had come at once. He checked Seymour's name with the Criminal Records Office, found he had several serious convictions, including one a year earlier, for the attempted murder of a woman – by strangulation. The charge had been reduced to attempted manslaughter and he had been bound over.

Seymour had written to Mrs Andrews from Hove – which was where he was now proved to be – and was tracked down. His ownership of the hammer was proved by Horwell who had soaked, what looked like breadcrumbs in Seymour's suitcase. They unrolled to reveal that they were scrapings of the identifying labels from the hammer which had been bought in an Oxford shop and used as a weapon on Mrs Kempson. The jury took 38 minutes to find him Guilty and, on 10 December, 1931 Henry Daniel Seymour was hanged in Oxford Prison.[10]

NOTES FOR CHAPTER FOURTEEN

1. *The Golden Age of Murder*, p195
2. *Bloody Murder, p107-8*
3. *The Golden Age of Murder,* p90
4. *Ibid*, p246-7
5. *Ibid*, p194
6. In fact London's murder rate *was* remarkably low. With a population of nearly eight million: in 1926 there were sixteen murders, the work of 14 persons and only one was unsolved. In 1927, there were 27 murders, all solved, the work of 23 persons – ten of whom committed suicide. In 1928, 21 murders, two by the same hand, 11 were arrested, seven committed suicide

and the 3 for whom no arrests were made were abortion cases. 'These figures,' wrote The Receiver, J F Moylan, 'explain why Scotland Yard has no "Homicide Bureau".' *Scotland Yard and the Metropolitan Police,* p176

7. *The Graphic,* 27 December 1930

8. *Hambrook of the Yard,* p237 -244.

9. *Ibid,* p206-236.

10. *Murder Squad* (Tom Tullett) p99-106

15

All Change?

In 1931 came the biggest shake up and shock to Scotland Yard since the appointment of Howard Vincent as Commissioner in 1897 following their corruption scandal. This time, however, the change was not primarily due to any police wrongdoing (although there had been a couple of scandals in the late Twenties[1]) but were largely the difficulties brought about by the passage of time and changing financial circumstances.

The problems were manifold. The dire economic situation brought about a constant demand for economies such as swingeing cuts in police numbers and pay at a time when there was an increase in the use of cars not only by criminals but the general public which, in turn, called for more traffic control via the new Road Traffic Acts. These required more police manpower and expensive innovations such as traffic signals and police boxes to help cope with the increasingly lethal traffic accidents in the capital (in 1928; 1,238 deaths and 54,461 injured[2]). It did not help that outdated beats and obsolete laws on often minor matters such as betting, which were still expected to be implemented, and they encouraged low level corruption. (The very first women police,[3] officially taken on in

1919 as Women Police Patrols, had been treated with extreme hostility by the male officers and when I was researching the first history of The British Women Police one of them told me that it was because the men didn't like the women seeing the wholesale bribery that went on.)

Public Order problems also weighed heavily due to Mosley and his Blackshirts, Communist spies and IRA threats. The editorial staff and the printers of *The Daily Worker* had been arrested on charges of incitement to Mutiny and the out-of-control Race Track Gangs were resorting to razors and guns.

Powers that be felt that the man to sort out these problems was the intolerant and autocratic Viscount Hugh Montague Trenchard who had solved the Royal Air Force post-war problems. He is now mostly known for doing for the police what the Golden Age crime novelists had long been doing – opening up the middle and upper ranks of the service to easy access by the educated upper classes and thus closing them off to the lower ranks.

The police founder Robert Peel had never wanted to employ 'gentlemen' as he thought they would be 'above their work'. Howard Vincent had wanted 'gentlemen of good education and social standing' but found that among the recruits they *did* get the best of them came from the farms and the worst from domestic service.

However, J F Moylan, the Receiver of the Metropolitan Police [Financial Manager] revealed that the policy pursued from the first days of the Metropolitan Police [Financial Manager] was to get men from the agricultural community both due to their superior physique (needed due to the long, hard hours, and to cope with violence) but also because countrymen without previous experience of town life would make more trustworthy policemen than those who were London bred 'and might be described as knowing too much about London.'

This became harder in about 1890 when, due to government regulations, conditions improved in the provincial forces and, in 1910, new regulations meant the Metropolitan Police had to give *their* men a day off a week, so they had to send out 'a small commission' to find the additional 16 hundred men required to do this. The best recruits proved to be from the West Country and the Scottish Highlands.

In 1919, after the armistice, they needed several thousand more men so they went recruiting among our army in France. Unfortunately, 'quality was rather sacrificed for quantity' and it was impossible to keep 'a considerable proportion' of these men afterwards.[4]

The education of potential recruits improved a little. However, in 1928, 30% of those applicants who were satisfactory in physique and good character still had to be rejected due to illiteracy. Those accepted were over 20 and under 27 years of age, at least 5'9" and able to pass the preliminary educational test which included arithmetic and dictation of part of a leading article from *The Times*.[5]

Trenchard thought that the current recruitment system still attracted brawn not brains. Interestingly, it had not *always* been lack of education and sophistication that had been found wanting but the way the new men carried themselves. Chief Inspector Albert Gooding, who was in charge of the new training school at Peel House back in 1907, explained this when justifying why the first week of their new course was devoted to drill.

to drill.

'This has been found necessary, as when the candidates first join they are a very mixed lot and in a great many instances fresh from the country, awkward in gait, manner and general bearing.' Half of their second week was given over to more Education Instruction (writing, spelling, composition, dictation, grammar, errors in speech and writing, use of maps, plans, etc.) The rest of the week covered Police Duty and more drill.[6]

Rather more sinisterly, J F Moylan revealed, 'Originally, a Metropolitan Police recruit, before being posted to duty, was given nothing but a week or two's drill at Wellington Barracks. This had the effect of reducing him to a state in which he was prepared to obey orders without question.'[7]

But at least Moylan grasped one reason why the police service was not an easy one for which to recruit. 'Much of an ordinary constable's work is characterised by monotonous performance of routine but at any time he may be called upon to exercise intelligence and discretion of a high order.'[8]

In other words, what many people overlooked, was that all the trickiest decisions and coping strategies were made by constables at the scene not those safely ensconced at the station or offices with easy means of accessing information and other opinions.

Percy Sillitoe, who had been making waves as the forward-looking Chief Constable of Sheffield City Police, where he had been sorting out the gang culture and improving police officer's working conditions and practices, did *not* see that it was essential that a police constable should be a man of more than average intelligence or that if his standard of education was higher than the next man's he would be a better policeman.

'Indeed,' he wrote in *Cloak Without Dagger*, ' I once argued with some passion on this point with Lord Trenchard. It was his opinion that if university graduates could be induced to join the police force, improved standards of police conduct would automatically result.'

Sillitoe abhorred the idea that these young men would then be trained as an officer class and join the police as Station Sub Inspectors. 'To me, it seemed absurd that these young men should be sent out as the superiors of Superintendents twice their age who often had a great fund of real knowledge acquired through their years of service, and who were now, as a result of this scheme, debarred from any chance of promotion beyond that rank.'[9]

The biggest joke of all was that Trenchard himself was so ill-educated that he was incapable of composing or dictating a coherent document. Nonetheless, he *did* appreciate that the Met needed shaking up, had some good ideas and carried out improvements in wireless communications, housing and canteen services – plus adding three more policewomen to the CID and establishing a Detective Training School[10].

In *1931* Sillitoe went on to an even tougher job as Chief Constable of Glasgow. He had started an embryo forensic lab in Sheffield and began to do the same in Glasgow as did Trenchard in the Met, and this was established in 1935, the year he retired.

Meanwhile, policing remained a dangerous job as Constables Pattenden and Collis discovered when on plain clothes duty guarding the pavilion of the Home Farm Lawn Tennis Club in Thames Ditton late one September night in 1931. Suddenly, two men approached and tried to force the door. Our gallant policemen sprang into action but, to their surprise, the thieves offered no resistance when they were arrested. Then, suddenly, P. C .Collis suffered a terrific blow to his head which felled him, leaving him senseless.

Pattenden struggled to control both the suspects, blowing his whistle as he did so. Then one of the men produced a pistol, aimed it directly at him and fired four shots. As the young constable fell the suspects took off, disappearing into the darkness while Collis, now roused, struggled to aid his injured colleague. First taking him to the local Cottage Hospital then, at speed, to St Thomas's.

What followed was reported as being the most intensive man-hunt since the murder of P.C. Gutteridge four years earlier. Superintendent Cornish, now one of the Big Four, ordered all Flying Squad vehicles to pick up any officers they could find to man the cordon thrown around the area. Next day, they were assisted by two volunteer airmen, flying low, whom the *Daily Herald* immediately dubbed *The Sky Sherlocks*.

Initially thought to have been be shot in the stomach, which could have been fatal at the time, the bullets were in fact found to have penetrated Pattenden's left arm and shoulder so did not prove life threatening but *did* result in him being in a serious condition for a while and eventually to his early retirement.

The suspects, 27 year-old kitchen porter Yaroslaw Charles, and 27-year-old labourer, Leonard William Short, were soon caught. Yaroslaw admitted he had fired the shots, was bitterly regretting it and was glad the constable had survived. He had fired only to frighten him. Then, somehow, had lost control. Much was made in court and the Press of our police being unarmed and of the necessity of maintaining that situation.

Prosecuting counsel pointed out that P C Pattenden was still in hospital and would be there for some time, suffering from a fractured collar bone, and wounds to the left shoulder-blade and neck and that the bullets had just missed his heart.

Charles, charged with attempted murder, insisted that he had no intention to murder but he was *not* helped by a manuscript found in his room which spoke of an imaginary hold-up of a booking clerk and continued: 'If I shot the clerk, if he resisted, should I be a murderer? Certainly not. It is in self-defence. He knows that if he resists or raises an alarm he is committing suicide, because I only shoot for the benefit of my own safety.' Charles claimed he had copied this from a journal.

The judge was not impressed and sentenced him to 15 years penal servitude, two years of it to be in hard labour.[11]

However, it was not just gunfire from which policemen were at risk. Motor cars continued to be a threat, not only from the bandits, but also from the general public who were still learning how to drive their cars and to obey traffic signals from police officers. (In 1920 there had been under 200,000 registered motor car users but, by 1930, there were over a million and in *that* year the 20 mile-an-hour limit was dropped.)

Writing in 1929, The Met Police Receiver, J F Moylan, revealed that regulating traffic had become much more dangerous. 'Metropolitan Policemen are knocked down and injured by motor vehicles to the number of about one every other day.'[12]

As well as members of the Met's Murder Squad being called in to assist other forces, their Fingerprint experts continued to be needed all over the country – the accuracy of fingerprints still having to be proved. Juries needed convincing by demonstrations and explanations from an expert – despite the science being accepted throughout the world.

Thus, experts from the Branch found themselves appearing for the prosecution in courts from one end of the country to another equipped with their magnifying glasses, enlarged photographs and weight of knowledge. They also became involved in some of the cases, being called to the scene to find the fingerprints. One longstanding member, Detective Inspector Fred Cherrill, even became adept in recognizing by sight the prints of regular offenders and, in 1931, he took the science a step further by introducing palm prints of a prolific burglar and convinced the judge and jury that they were as immutable as fingerprints.

In his book, *Cherrill of the Yard,* he describes how he became involved in the onward progression of one convoluted case which began one August Sunday morning in 1933 when Mrs Charles Fox was woken by the sound of breaking glass coming from downstairs in their little home in West Bromwich. She woke her husband who, with the aid of a candle, ventured to investigate. Suddenly, his candlelight was extinguished, there were sounds of a scuffle and a groan. Her husband struggled back upstairs, tried to say something, then slithered to the floor and died in her arms, a bowie-knife embedded in his back.

Mrs Fox rushed to the window, flung it open and screamed for help. A workman on his way home heard her calls and ran into the High Street where he found two policemen. It turned out that Fox had suffered seven knife wounds. It also turned out that it was to be a busy night in West Bromwich. During the early hours someone broke into a butcher's shop, stole a few pounds in cash and settled down to wash himself, leaving the water in a bowl; used the butchers safety razor to shave, leaving the lather on the razor then got a needle and cotton out of a cupboard and apparently carried out some running repairs leaving the threaded needle under the grill, before taking a swig from a bottle of milk.

The bottle was sent to Scotland Yard and within a few minutes Cherrill telephoned the West Bromwich Police to say that the prints were those of one Stanley Eric Hobday, whose record was in the files at the Yard. He was also known to the West Bromwich police but, unsurprisingly, he was not at home.

Then, for the first time in the criminal history of the UK, radio was used to broadcast the description of a man whom the police wanted to interview in connexion with a murder and police throughout the country were notified.

It was becoming clear that Hobday had had an even busier night than they had imagined.

It seemed that shortly after leaving the butchers, where he had stopped for his ablutions, he had stolen a motor car – a Jowett Javelin. An Irish farm-labourer working on a farm over sixty miles from West Bromwich heard the car crashing then saw it do a complete somersault. Inside the car was found a suitcase but no driver.

Meanwhile, the broadcasts were having the desired effect. A worker, driving some cows across a lane as far North as near Carlisle, saw a man who answered the description being spread abroad. He held a hankie over his face as though to prevent recognition. The farmhand told his employer, who phoned the police, and PC Elder of the Cumbria Constabulary was soon speeding in their direction.

Near Gretna Green the constable spied a tired and hungry-looking man picking blackberries and when he asked his name he said 'Hobday'. He'd had enough. At the police station after an identification parade his first request was, 'Can I have a banana.'

Since the window of the victim's house was very small and the footprints in the soil outside were of a small size four it had been surmised that Hobday himself must be very small and indeed he was. Plaster casts were made of the footprints and they corresponded with his feet. The black cotton, repairing a tear in the left sleeve of his jacket, was identical with that found in the needle left at the butchers – each piece being composed of six strands. The lather he left after shaving at the butchers contained hairs that proved identical to the ones obtained when he was shaved in prison.

As for the suitcase – well he had lost it, hadn't he, after he had been required to leave a campsite. In fact, he said, he had hidden it in the woods but when he went to collect it, it was gone. But what had been in it? He mentioned the tent, cooking utensils and the knife. When found and opened only the knife was missing. His defence, of course, was that it was not *he* who had retrieved the suitcase and, subsequently, left the knife embedded in Mr Fox's back, then stolen the motor car. Alas, Hobday's fingerprints were found on the car's starting handle and the milk bottle from the butcher's shop.

Cherrill, seeing the absolutely bereft wife in the witness box wondered just why Hobday had chosen *their* house and learned that Fox supplemented his earnings by collecting for the National Clothing Company and on the afternoon before his death had collected fourteen shillings which, it seemed,

Hobday had heard about.

Hobday's lawyer, Sir Reginald Coventry K.C., did not call any defence witnesses claiming that the case had not been proved. Who could believe that after foully murdering another human and his hands still bearing the stains of blood anyone could calmly go off and do all the things they claimed?

'It is a fantastic story – one such as the author of a 'penny-dreadful' would consider so ridiculous and unreal that he would never find a publisher for it.'

A publisher might not have bought the story but the jury did despite Coventry's rapier-like attack on Cherrill's evidence. Hobday was found Guilty and hanged.[13]

NOTES FOR CHAPTER FIFTEEN

1. The year of 1928 had been a particularly bad one due to what were known as The Gentlemen in the Park Cases (hanky panky on park benches with a young ladies) in one of which two constables arrested Sir Leo Money a well-known economist. The case had been dismissed at magistrates court leading to accusations of a cover up. Chief Inspector Collins, charged with investigating, was accused of improper behaviour whilst questioning Miss Savidge, the young lady in question. Much was made of this but the case advanced the cause of women police one of whom, from thence forward, had always to be present on such interviews. Lilian Wyles, the policewoman who *had* been present, saved the day for Chief Inspector Collins because (judging by her comments in her autobiography) she had been a little economical with the truth when questioned about his handling of the case.

The other scandal that year concerned another sign of the times – the popularity of night clubs – which were seen by some as an antidote to the recent horrors of war. It seemed that a Police Sergeant Goddard who had been given the job of helping to clean them up, was found (via anonymous letters to the Yard) to own a £2,000 house, an expensive Chrysler motor car and a well-stocked safety deposit box which, given his weekly wage of £6, appeared a little suspicious. Wensley investigated and, eventually, the sergeant earned eighteen months hard labour. Interestingly, this case did not appear in Wensley's memoirs.

2. *Scotland Yard and The Metropolitan Police* by J F Moylan C.B., p247

3. Called Women Police Patrols they were not sworn in nor given a power of arrest so made ineffective due to the limitation of their work and powers. *The British Policewoman: Her Story,* p84-5

4. *Scotland Yard and The Metropolitan Police,* p 98-99.

5. *Ibid, p103*

6. *Training the Metropolitan Policeman: A Historical Survey from 1829-1910. (The Training School Magazine* No 44, 1963)

7. *Scotland Yard and the Metropolitan Police,* p102

8. *Ibid* p99-100

9. *Cloak Without Dagger,* p79-80

10. *The Official Encyclopedia of Scotland Yard,* p267

11. *Daily Herald, 24 September, 1931; Illustrated Police News,* 10 October, 1931; *The Times,* 9 October 1931.

12. *Scotland Yard and the Metropolitan Police,* p286.

13. *Cherrill of the Yard,* p104-112.

16

The Branch

Whilst the crimes of the murderers, motor bandits and race track gangs, and the traffic problems, were ebbing and flowing, the officers of the Yard's Special Branch had other things on their minds such as the unlawful activities of the Communist Party of Great Britain (CPGB) and the Irish Republican Army (IRA).

The Special Branch, which was an offshoot of the CID, had been established following the bombing activities of the Fenians in Britain during the 1880s. Since then, the Branch had kept an eye on Indian Nationalists, Suffragettes, German spies, Fascist Black Shirts, Anarchists, Nihilists, the CPGB. and the IRA. However, since the murder of Field Marshal Sir Henry Wilson in June 1922, the IRA and Fenians had been preoccupied with activities back in Ireland.[1]

In May, 1921, the Branch had made an attempt to restrain the Communist Party of Great Britain by raiding their headquarters and seizing 3 tons of literature held to be subversive since it advocated violence, claiming that one class of the Community should be armed to overawe the others – engage in civil war in fact. The accused were sentenced to six months hard labour and the printers fined £200 with costs and were obliged to make an undertaking never again to print that sort of literature.[2]

The Branch officers were thought to have more in common with the sophisticated, presentable, educated detectives of fiction than some of their CID colleagues – although, in fact, some of them had progressed on from the CID, others directly from the uniformed branch. Knowledge of foreign languages helped admission, as did shorthand, for the taking down of fiery seditious speeches.

Some of their work, such as guarding Royalty, did appear glamorous. As well as our own Royalty they took care of visiting Kings and Queens, and their offspring. Long-serving Detective Inspector Fitch, who spoke many languages, even numbered a Czar, an Empress and a Shah among his numerous previous foreign Royal charges and wrote fulsomely about most of them but admitted some trepidation when it came to dealing with the impulsive whims of Kaiser William II sensing 'he had it in him to cause great difficulties'.[3]

Harold Brust, who moved into the Special Branch from the CID, describes some of the requirements for guarding the top people as being shrewd, courageous and quick acting. He also asked, 'Can he stand on the fringe of a knot of Cabinet Ministers for instance, ready for any emergency, yet merged into that group by reason of his mien, speech, and general deportment?'[4]

Of course aspects of Special Branch work could be tedious and trying – keeping watch at airports and ports for undesirable aliens – guarding important persons who did not want to be guarded – tailing suspects night and day – and being ready at a moment's notice to dash off who knows where.

One day, in 1924, Brust received a typical urgent summons to headquarters. On arrival, his chief told him, 'Get ready to fly to Paris immediately,' handing him a file to study carefully *en route*. This contained information that an attempt might be made to attack Mr Austen Chamberlain the Foreign Secretary, whom he was to protect.

'He is at Versailles' Brust was told, 'and may proceed to Geneva to attend a meeting of the League of Nations, afterwards going on to Rome. The French Secret Service will help you, and arrangements will be made for you to have adequate help from the Italian police when you cross the border.'

Brust collected his emergency suitcase and dashed off to Croydon Airport where a plane was awaiting him.

The file revealed there was a gang of Egyptian students, already responsible for the death of Sir Lee Stack, Governor General of Anglo Egyptian Sudan, who now had their sights on Mr Chamberlain. Brust thought The Foreign Secretary difficult to miss being known for 'his orchid, his eyeglass, his top-hat, his calm, austere face, his unruffled mien'.

He located Mr Chamberlain in Versaille but found him most averse to protective surveillance. 'Quite frankly,' he told Brust, 'I believe that the more openly and freely one moves about, the less one has to fear. I myself, am quite indifferent. I do not think there will be any danger, and I do not like going about under guard.' Eventually however, they reached an agreement as to minimum arrangements.

On arrival in Geneva Brust had a conference with the Chief of Police and learned that one of the Egyptian students had been detained by them but was later informed that trace had been lost of the most lethal of the suspects who was 'a travelling trouble centre'. Nonetheless, they managed to exit Geneva without any drama, Brust remaining anxious about their forthcoming journey to Rome.

This began with him sitting in the next compartment to Chamberlain so that he could keep an eye on movement in the corridor. When they reached the Italian border he asked that the wagon-lit compartment occupied by the Foreign Secretary be vacated but the labels left on the windows and doors. He and Chamberlain would walk along to another (unlabelled) compartment where they would both sit. Brust asked that Italian detectives, who had been allocated to them at the border, be posted at intervals along the train and tell him of the slightest degree of anything suspicious.

One of the detectives soon reported that there was a man in the uniform of a train official who 'was doing something' to doors of the compartment they had just left. It turned out he was *not* a genuine train official and, after a struggle, was taken in charge. When they arrived in Rome they were assigned no less than forty Italian detectives for guard duty. Mussolini, (whom Brust met and was impressed by) was guarded continually by three hundred Secret Service men due to the constant attempts on his life.

Our Special Branch man was still deeply anxious but breathed more easily after being informed that a suspect had been taken into custody after being seen emerging from a restaurant doorway and rushing across the pavement as Chamberlain's car approached. The suspect *was* an Egyptian, answered the description of the suspect, had a loaded revolver in his pocket, but refused to talk.

Unsurprisingly, Brust was 'considerably relieved' when the

visit ended and they could go back home[5].

In 1925 the Special Branch went the whole hog and applied for warrants to enable them to arrest the entire Executive of the Communist Party of Great Britain for sedition. What was uncovered on their subsequent raid was, as expected, documents describing methods of undermining the authority of the State and ultimately destroying it, and undermining the authority of the Army officer class. Also, put forward in evidence, were their *Workers Weekly* articles suggesting methods of paralysing industry and advising readers to fraternise with soldiers in order to convince them that they must only use their arms on behalf of their class – and so on.

When the 12 defendants appeared at Bow Street Police Court on 23 October, 1925, they were greeted by a crowd, one of whom was carrying a red flag. A photograph in the *Daily Herald* the next day showed 'The police charging the crowd' to remove the flag and reported that several eye-witnesses said 'that the charge was uncalled for and alleged that the police used unnecessary force for their action.'[6] (But then the *Daily Herald was* a left wing newspaper and at one stage was nearly acquired by the Soviet Union.[7])

The same day, *The Illustrated London News* gave over a full page of photographs of the defendants plus one of a hundred strong crowd who 'sang *The Red Flag* during the court proceedings'. Also, a photograph of 'friends and wives of arrested Communist leaders . . . on the occasion of the Bow Street proceedings' who were looking so remarkably cheerful that they could have been on a jolly day out.

In evidence, various members of the Special Branch described a CPGB member's highly inflammatory 'harangue' during a demonstration in Trafalgar Square; the accused's visits to the Communist International in Moscow the previous year, and gave evidence to indicate that the party was financially supported by the Soviet Union. Correspondence produced discussed the possible usefulness of getting some Party Members into the Police in a big city such as Glasgow and a policy of exposing the real nature of the State and ultimately destroying it. Also a pamphlet telling members of the armed forces never to turn their guns onto their own class but onto the aggressor.[8]

All were convicted. Five of them (Pollit, Inkpin, Hannington, Gallagher and Rust) 'who had previous political convictions' were sentenced to 12 months imprisonment. The others were given the choice of either being bound over if they consented to having nothing more to do with Communism and its doctrines or six months in prison. Six of them chose the latter.[9]

In 1931, under the Westminster Treaty, it was decided that the Communists should be left to MI5 to deal with and that the Yard's Special Branch should just keep an eye on the IRA. After all, the latter was an area in which the police were most experienced and the subversive activities of the CPGB were now too big and International for them to handle.[10]

Given the lull due to IRA members involvement in the Spanish Civil War and that, under The Anglo-Irish Agreement of 1938, the Irish Government had been granted the remaining UK naval bases they wanted in Ireland and had been assured that they could remain neutral in a future war. Also, that the IRA in London were undergoing an internal power struggle so, all in all, it looked like the The Branch had got the best part of the deal and they could relax.[11]

Big mistake.

Few murder cases proved more curious than that of Charles Frederick Field and Norah Upchurch. In 1931 Field was a workman employed as a sign fitter on some empty shops in Shaftsbury Avenue. He had the keys and was the last person to have used them so when prostitute Norah Upchurch's body was found there he became an obvious suspect. But, he told a tale of handing the keys over to a man with an order to view who was wearing plus fours and had a gold tooth. However, a man he actually identified had no gold tooth but fortunately for Field, the Coroner's jury returned an open verdict.

The case remained unsolved until July, 1933, when Field suddenly confessed saying he had taken Norah to the shop to have sex but she had bitten him and he had lost his temper and gripped her throat – she had seemed to faint and he couldn't remember what happened next. He was charged with her murder but in court he pleaded Not Guilty and his account, not being consistent with the facts, meant he was acquitted and released. But what had *really* happened was that he had first confessed to a newspaper with the aim of getting some money for his story and the assurance that, should he be charged, they would pay for his defence. His ploy had worked.

In 1936 he tried the stunt again. He confessed to the murder of a middle-aged widow, Beatrice Vilna Sutton, who had been found dead in her flat due to suffocation. He had killed her, he declared, because he wanted to commit suicide but could not bring himself to do it but thought the murder would achieve that end. At his trial he withdrew his confession but this time the evidence against him was too strong and he was found Guilty and executed.[12] At the final moment, however he was almost upstaged by Mrs Van der Elst with her latest demonstration against the death penalty.

It may have been the financial situation in the 1930s which encouraged the idea of suicide as a way out of personal troubles or perhaps getting someone else to be surrogate. Certainly this appealed to commercial traveller Alfred Arthur Rouse, whose job facilitated his vigorous sexual life, but he had begun to feel overwhelmed by his number of illegitimate children and paternity orders.

Things came to a head when two young men returning from a Bonfire Night Party Dance near Northampton saw a bright glow in a hedgerow and a man climbing out of a ditch on the opposite side of the road. 'Looks as if someone had had a bonfire' commented the man on leaving.

On closer inspection, the glow turned out to be that of a blazing car with flames now reaching fifteen feet. When the police arrived and the fire had subsided they found a charred body sprawled across the front seats.

The number plate was still readable so the ownership of his Morris Minor was soon traced to Mr Rouse at his address in Finchley, North London. He was not at home but his wife claimed to have seen him at 1am that morning and, when shown scraps of clothing found on the corpse, she agreed that they looked like those of her husband.

Whilst this was happening, Arthur was visiting Ivy Jenkins in Wales who was about to give birth to his latest illegitimate child. But the newspapers were now full of pictures of the burnt out car which the girl's father showed Rouse who hurriedly boarded a bus for London. Instead of the Met having to proceed to a force to deal with one of their cases this one had been brought to them as they welcomed Rouse at the Hammersmith bus terminal.

Rouse claimed to be very relieved to be able to tell them all about it. He had picked up a hitch-hiker, he said, on the Great North Road just this side of St Albans. As they were approaching Northampton he had felt a call of nature and had gone off to relieve himself, after instructing his passenger to fill up the petrol tank from the can. No sooner had he got his pants down then he saw that the car was on fire. He rushed back and tried to open the car door but it was stuck – the hitch-hiker had mentioned having a smoke before he had left him . . .

However, at his trial in Northampton, Spilsbury mentioned petrol-soaked scraps of material on the body; an injury to the man's head and a piece of wood to which hairs were attached and that the man was probably alive when the fire took hold. Then there was evidence of the carburettor having been tampered with and Rouse making a bad impression in court due to his boastfulness and arrogance. He was found Guilty and hanged – but first he confessed. Like many murderers he clearly felt the need to be sure they got the details right. He described how he had strangled the nameless stranger, poured petrol over him, loosened the petrol union joint, taken the top off the carburettor, run a trail of petrol to the car – and set alight to it. The crime became a very famous one – his image as a lothario adding to its interest. It certainly affected the make-up of his jury, on which two women had been empanelled but were promptly removed after the Defence objected to their presence.[13] Despite the failure of some of these headline cases they still appeared to plant ideas in others heads – perhaps convincing people they could avoid their errors.

People such as Builder and Decorator Samuel Furnace. He had rented a shed as an office in the backyard of a Mr Wynne near Camden Town Underground Station when, on the evening of 3 January, 1933, a startled Mr Wynne saw the bed was on fire. When the blaze was extinguished the body of Mr Furnace was found sitting at his desk with a note beside him saying, 'Goodbye all. No work. No money. Sam J. Furnace.' A tenant of Furnace duly identified the body but his life insurance was declared void due to his suicide. Nonetheless the insurance company agreed to provide the widow with a generous grant. A satisfactory conclusion all round considering.

However, the Coroner, Mr Bentley Purchase, was *not* happy. He examined the body thoroughly and, after finding what appeared to be a bullet hole in the corpse's back and teeth more suitable for a younger man, concluded that *this* was *not* Samuel Furnace. When a full post mortem revealed a second bullet hole; that the victim had probably been dead *before* being set on fire; that a sodden post office savings book belonging to Walter Spatchett, aged twenty-five, was found in the overcoat pocket; Purchase knew he was right. *And* Spatchett and Furnace were known to be acquainted.

A nationwide hunt was instituted, the BBC announced that the missing man was wanted for murder and, like the Pembridge Square murderer, he was traced to Southend (after making the mistake of writing a letter to his brother in law arranging a means of meeting). The person he met was Superintendent Cornish who had arrested Jacoby all those years ago and was now one of the Big Five.

Like Rouse, Furnace explained how it had all been a terrible accident. He had been showing Spatchett the gun and the young man cocked it even though it was loaded. It went off and shot him. Furnace lost his head – didn't know what to do – then the idea of making him a stand-in occurred.

In *Murders of the Black Museum* Gordon Honeycombe wonders whether Furnace's story would have been believed in court. There was no way of knowing as he committed suicide in his cell. After complaining of the cold he had been brought his overcoat which, it turned out, had not been searched. There happened to be a bottle of hydrochloric acid hidden in the pocket. Nonetheless, the Coroner's jury found him guilty of murder in his absence.

NOTES FOR CHAPTER SIXTEEN

1. *The Branch*, p94
2. *Ibid*, p79
3. *Memoirs of a Royal Detective*, p209
4. *In Plain Clothes*, p27-28
5. *Ibid*, p46-50
6. *Daily Herald*, 24 October, 1925; *The Branch*, p80-83
The *Daily Herald* was nearly acquired by the Soviet Union after it found itself broke in August 1920. British Intelligence intercepted a telegram sent by a Bolshevik diplomat in London to Lenin in Moscow telling him that he had paid the paper £40.000.00 and would be giving them a further £10.000.00. Wikipedia: *Daily Herald (United Kingdom)*.
7. *The Branch*, p80-83
8. *Liverpool University Press Online: Raid on HQ of CPGB 1925*
9. *Illustrated London News*, 12 October 1925

10. *The Branch*, p94-96

11. *Ibid*, p95-96

12. *Murderers Who's Who*, p131-2 and p281-2

13. 'Rouse Bans Women on Jury', *The Daily Herald*, 27 January 1931.

17

Very Private Detectives

In 1932 a woman sergeant was appointed to assist the solitary female figure of Inspector Lilian Wyles in the Metropolitan Police CID, and three female constables were attached to the CID at West End Central to be trained to assist in statement taking.

By contrast there was already a plethora of *fictional* woman detectives who had emerged, not from the pens of the Golden Age writers, but from writers as far back 1864, arriving on the scene when the first suggestions of female equality began creeping in. The first was *The Female Detective*, by Andrew Forrest, and the second, *Revelations of a Lady Detective*, by William Stephens Hayward.[1]

The latter is particularly startling for the time in that on the book's cover our lady detective is shown brazenly blowing forth the smoke from her cigarette while she coquettishly lifts her skirt. And she carries a colt revolver and handles cases such as murder and kidnapping. Small wonder a recent Amazon review from *Past Offences* on the British Library reprint of the book begins with, 'An absolute blast from beginning to end . . .'

Of course, all these ladies were *Private* Detectives. From

1860s onwards several amateurs feature in the 'sensation novels'[2] and in monthly journals such as *The Strand*. Another influx of fictional female private detectives began in *1893 with* such as *The Experiences of Loveday Brooke, Lady Detective,* by Catherine Louisa Perkis.

Loveday is a 'lady' whose has defied convention by becoming a private detective which cuts her off sharply from her former associates. She does not rely on women's intuition in her work but, according to the late Dr Chris Willis who was an authority on such matters, 'she deduces facts from clues in the manner of Sherlock Holmes'. As Chris points out, the fictional 19th-century female private detectives were nearly always middle class, young, pretty, and single – leaving openings for romantic possibilities. Many were also university educated but had found the traditional graduate professions barred to them due to their gender – as had their writers if they were female.

Loveday, is an exception regarding appearance (possibly as she is the creation of a woman) being 'neither handsome nor ugly' and having 'nonedescript' features[3].

However, two of the most popular fictional female detectives at that time, were the 'sweet and womanly' Dorcas Dene, who was obliged to take up the work to support her blind husband, and Miss Cayley, 'a lady of considerable personal attractions'. Both were written by men. The first was the work of the social reformer George R Sims, and the second by Canadian, Grant Allen, who believed in equality in marriage and wrote another with a female detective, *Hilda Wade,* which was published after his death in 1899 his friend Conan Doyle having finished the final episode for him.[4]

In 1910, from the Hungarian Baroness Orczy, came the

short stories featuring *Lady Molly of Scotland Yard*, a character who was to be heartily disapproved of by D L Sayers because Lady Molly relied on female intuition to make her deductions. She wasn't that popular with the fictional policemen either. They were shocked that a murder case should be in the hands of the 'female department'[5] although she *was* only working there in order to rescue her husband whom she thought had been wrongly convicted of murder and gave it up as soon as her mission had been accomplished. This insistence on the female detectives having been driven into the unladylike position of doing a man's job was another requirement for being accepted by readers.

In 1889 the popular weekly magazine *Titbits* published five features about woman private detectives under the banner title: *Queer Feminine Occupations.*[6] They examined all aspects of the job including women's superior powers of observation and how the private detective agencies had long realised the necessity of employing women 'on certain delicate missions'. They also revealed what a well paid job it could be although Chris Willis did wonder whether these fees were somewhat exaggerated.

In reality policeman's wives had always been called upon when only a woman would do for undercover work and occasionally even some genuine female private detectives were utilised by the police as well. They were now operating alongside such wonders as Lady Photographers, Lady Farmers, Lady Gardeners and even Lady Balloonists.

Of course, one of the real reasons women were needed, at least for undercover work, was that people did not expect to see them in that role. Serving as a uniformed officer in the West End in the 1950s I was quite often pulled off my shift to accompany CID or Clubs officers because operating alone they were too obvious.

Indeed, on one occasion, after a late turn duty, following which I was in a party waiting to raid a night club, an urgent call came from the two male officers doing the observation at the club. They had sensed they were attracting too much attention and were worried that the raid might fall through. Rapid attempts were made by my colleagues to add a touch of glamour to my everyday civvies with dangly earrings and such, so I could be rushed in there to meet up with them, have a dance or two, and thus save the day – which we did.[7]

Lilian Wyles had only been allowed into the Metropolitan Police CID in 1920 mainly to take sex offence statements – in other words from victims of rape and sexual assault – which after the Savidge Affair the men had realised could be dynamite for them. The next three CID women were housed at West End Central and one of these, Amy Ettridge, was later to do very well and make a name for herself in some interesting cases.

Following the passing of the risibly-named Sex Disqualification (Removal) Act in 1922 some CID openings also occurred in other forces. Most markedly, in the Lancashire Constabulary where the Chief Constable Sir Phillip Lane, who disapproved of women in uniform without proper powers, took no less than sixteen policewomen and four Specials into the CID. It did turn out they mainly dealt with women and children, kept and collated records, took statements in shorthand and did a little undercover work where a woman was less conspicuous. (There is a delightful photograph of Sir Phillip looking like a Sultan amidst his bevy of lady detectives.)

As for Golden Age amateur lady detectives, in her second

book, *The Secret Adversary*, Agatha Christie featured the light-hearted sleuthing pair Tommy and Tuppence. Then, in 1930, after a trial run of six short stories in which Miss Jane Marple was pitted against various characters, she was judged to be a strong enough to take the detective lead in a novel: *Murder at the Vicarage.*

At her launch Miss Marple was sixty-five to seventy years old and, though cheerful and kind, had one outstanding characteristic which she shared with Agatha's grandmother – that she always expected the worst of everybody.[8]

The book was serialised in several newspapers from *The Daily Mail,* to some local papers such as *The Staffordshire Evening Sentinel* and *The Dundee Evening Telegraph* under the heading:

Who Killed Colonel Prothero?
by Agatha Christie
*A Murder mystery that **you** can solve.*

THE CLUES

Seven people are suspected of committing a murder in a country vicarage.

The first clue is in the first dozen lines, and all clues necessary to the solution of the mystery are given before the final chapter.

Give your powers of observation and deduction a test, and discover who killed Colonel Prothero before Agatha Christie tells you.

(Another Instalment Tomorrow.)

As for the reviewers, one of them felt that the author had 'made many bricks with little straw' and that 'in less skilful hands these village dwellers might easily have proved boring in the extreme'[9]. Another rued the absence of Christie's 'little detective Poirot'.[10,] A third gave the new female sleuth only passing attention merely noting: 'it is left for an observant spinster to carry off the detective honours and put the local police on the right track' and, complained about the number of suspects saying, 'One can have too much mystery in a book of this kind.'[11]

Interestingly enough the author agreed with the latter. As she said in her autobiography, she was not so pleased with it as she had been at the time. It had far too many characters, and too many sub plots. 'But at any rate the *main* plot is sound.'[12]

In *Masters of Mystery,* H D Thomson points out that Miss Marple would only be able solve murder problems on her native heath and that if the author intended a future for Miss Marple 'she will be bound to find this an exasperating limitation'.

As Martin Edwards pointed out, 'Like so many other people, Thomson under-rated Christie. She proved more than equal to the challenge.'[13]

In 1933 three new members were elected to membership of the Detection Club two of whom were out of the usual run. They were Anthony Gilbert, which was a pen name of Lucy Beatrice Malleson, and E R Punshon.

Of course, it was not unusual for female writers to adopt male pseudonyms in the hope of being taken more seriously but in this genre, at this time, women writers seemed to be doing well just being female. Nonetheless, as Anthony Gilbert, Lucy Beatrice produced over 60 crime novels, most of which featured Arthur Crook, a vulgar London Lawyer of doubtful ethics. She also wrote many short stories and radio plays and even invented a phoney male biography for herself.

E R Punshon had produced five novels with an Inspector Carter and Sergeant Bell of Scotland Yard, characterised as a 'tortoise and hare team', but in *Information Received* (1933) came P C Bobby Owen, who was to stay for thirty-five more novels as she gradually climbed through the ranks. The author himself had come up the hard way, having left school at fourteen – so he broke the current Oxbridge hold on the Detection Club membership.

The third of the trio was Gladys Mitchell, London University educated, with a chief character of Mrs Bradley, who was a psychoanalyst and author, and delved into more unconventional subjects such as Freudian psychology and witchcraft. She, too, used male pseudonyms in some other writings.

NOTES FOR CHAPTER SEVENTEEN

1. Another reviewer has a different opinion: Amazon Review *Vine Voice (2020)* 'Disappointing'. Disputes its being the first, citing Penny Dreadfuls as a more likely source.
Amazon Review ****Past Offences (2020)
2. Sensation novels have been described as 'romance and realism' in a way that 'strains both modes to the limit'. *A Companion Guide to the Victorian Novel*, p261
3. The Female Sherlock, p4-5
4. Wikipedia: Biography: Death and posthumous publication
5. The Female Sherlock, p10

6. *Titbits:* 14 December, 1889; 20 September 1890; and 18 April 1891

7. *Lady Policeman,* p96

8. *Agatha Christie's Autobiography,* p450

9. *The Yorkshire Post,* 24 November, 1930

10. *The Western Morning News,* 13 October,1930

11. *Sheffield Daily Telegraph,* 13 November, 1930

12. *Agatha Christie Autobiography,* p449

13. *The Golden Age of Murder,* p155

18
The Female of the Species

In 1934 in came New Zealander Ngaio Marsh with her novel *A Man Lay Dead* in which Detective Superintendent Roderick Alleyn, made his debut. He was another gentleman cop thus having the benefit of the two angles – partially the fictional gloss and partially the element of reality which was starting to creep into detective fiction[1]. The latter was probably partly due to the writers inviting some real-life detectives into their social lives and also to the new focus on forensics.

Ngaio, the daughter of a bank clerk, had studied painting at Canterbury College in New Zealand, then joined a theatre company as an actress. The theatre and art were to feature in much of her work but Julian Symons felt her strengths were in revealing the amusing undercurrents beneath ordinary social intercourse and that she became rather dull when it came to the handling of the investigation.

As we saw, Agatha Christie used her experiences working in a hospital medical dispensary in the Great War to use death by poisoning as her means of murder in her first detective novel, *The Mysterious Affair at Styles,* the surprise solution depending on her knowledge of the properties of strychnine[2].

Arsenic had been the favourite poison in early Victorian times due to its easy availability and lack of an appropriate test to indicate its presence in a body. That was discovered in 1836 by James Marsh and, in 1851 the Arsenic Act of 1851, was brought in to help control the poison and make it less accessible. Nonetheless, arsenic remained something of a favourite, particularly with women.

One of the strangest poisoning cases the Yard men had had to deal with was the one to which Detective Chief Inspector Keech and Detective Sergeant Thorpe were called in to at Coventry in the Spring of 1934. The situation could not have been more different from that in *The Mysterious Affair at Styles.*

The victim was Mrs Mary Jane Cole, wife of a sandblaster, to whom a doctor had been called five days earlier. She had been rushed to hospital but was found dead on arrival.

By now, some Provincial police forces were becoming more adept at handling the first stages of murder enquiries themselves thus, in this instance, the local sergeant had taken statements from the husband, who was off sick. From the son, he had taken away the glass from which Mary had been drinking and from the mortuary he had acquired the half a quartern [a quarter] of whisky which been taken there with her and which proved to contain traces of arsenic.

Initially, suicide seemed to be the obvious motive but when a couple of Coventry's detectives learned that Mrs Cole had been having an affair with Harry Sinclair, a night-watchman in a nearby ironworks, their investigations widened. The Yard man went first to see the obvious suspect – the husband – who told them that she had been a good wife and mother until five years ago when she had taken to drink. He blamed the bad company she had fallen into while queuing up at the labour exchange to draw his unemployment benefit – then she had become infatuated with Harry Sinclair.

She had been seen at the ironworks at night with Sinclair and constantly at pubs during the day so obviously the affair was not a secret one. This, and her drunkenness, had caused marital quarrels which had sometimes come to blows although recently, due to his poor health and for the sake of their children, the husband had just put up with it. Indeed, on the day of her death, they had been out together to a pub where, in the afternoon, she had seen the night-watchman before going home to get the family meal ready. Then husband and wife had gone out together again. Mr Cole had taken with him the quartern bottle which he had intended to get filled with whisky but it had been forgotten until they were on their way home when she volunteered to go back and get it filled.

The Yard men set about establishing Mary Jane's movements until her eventual arrival home and found she had spent all the time in the *White Hart* public house with the night-watchman but the licensee insisted that the bottle had not been filled there. *The Oak*, and the wine and spirit shop of Waters & Co, also drew a blank although the bottle *was* wrapped in brown paper of the type used by the latter. After getting home she had left the bottle on the table then gone out again to get some faggots. While out, she had a glass of beer at *The Oak* but had *not* joined the watchman although she had known he was in there.

The Coles's sons were, unsurprisingly, strict teetotallers so only her husband was likely to touch the whisky which he now did, took a sip and spat it out, called for water and became close to collapse. A son helped him upstairs to bed. When Mary Jane returned home her husband warned her that the whisky 'tasted funny' and *not* to drink it but she finished off most of the glass and agreed it *did* taste funny. She told her son to empty the bottle down the drain, which he did, and washed and wiped the glass. She then collapsed, and by the time the doctor arrived, she was dead. Her body smelled of almonds, indicating cyanide, so the Chief Constable had made the call to the Yard.

Under the Poisons and Pharmacy Act, 1908, there were strict regulations about the sale of preparations containing cyanide. It could only be sold by Registered Chemists and Druggists and to someone they either knew or had been introduced by someone they knew and all these details were entered into a Poisons Book, with reasons for sale and labelled with the name and address of the seller and the word POISON writ large[3].

Presuming that *Mary Jane* had put the poison in the bottle, where had she got it? Much time and effort was spent following her possible movements that evening by the Coventry Police and Keech and Thorpe. En route they had discovered that it proved to be not potassium cyanide but sodium cyanide which was used in enormous quantities in the city's many engineering works including the one for which the night-watchman worked and *he* had access to the poison. But had she?

The analyst, who told them that the cyanide in the whisky bottle had been sufficient to kill thirteen people, now informed them that there were traces of it in her purse.

Keech and Thorpe thought this was becoming interesting

They came to the conclusion that Mrs Cole had decided dispose of her husband and that, when she left the poisoned whisky on the table, she knew very well that husband was the only one of the family who would touch it and that she came home from her last visit to the public house expecting to find him dead. When he wasn't, but the poisoned whisky had been revealed, she had lost her head and drank the glass.

The night-watchman revealed that Mary Jane *had* said she would like to live with him but would *not* do so while her husband was alive. Now *his* statements were becoming ambiguous and, instead of returning to see them as arranged, he went to a solicitor and also gave a statement to the *Weekly Dispatch*. He had, he admitted, taken some cyanide home with him but only to deal with wasp nests. He had never given any to Mrs Cole but admitted she *could* have picked some up at the works where, up until about twelve months earlier, there had always been some loose in a tray in the plating shop. Even now, the night watchman always had access to the poison store.

And it appeared she may have made a previous attempt on her husband twelve days earlier when, at 10.30 in the morning, she had taken him some tea, after which he had spent the day in pain. She had not returned home until 10.30pm that day when she was brought home helplessly drunk.

There was no proof that Sinclair, the night-watch-man, had persuaded her nor assisted a plan to kill her husband. The Coroner's jury's verdict was that the poison was self-administered; that it had been supplied by Sinclair, but that he had not put it into the whisky.[4]

It seemed that women in the Provinces were tiring of their spouses. At least that was the impression when, on 26 May, 1934, soon after the case of Mrs Cole, an anonymous letter was received by Inspector Dodson of the Lincolnshire Police.

It alleged that, despite the cause of death of a Mr Major being given as epilepsy, the recently-widowed Mrs Major had in fact poisoned her lorry driver husband. Why, the letter asked, had he complained of his food tasting so nasty that he had thrown it to the neighbour's dog which had also died jerking and stiffening so quickly. Years before, the letter-writer had heard Ethel Major threatening to kill her husband.

Inspector Dodson checked with the doctor who had issued the death certificate when Arthur had died following an attack of violent spasms and muscular contractions but, since he had not attended Mr Major before, he had accepted the wife's word that for years he had suffered from fits. However, after a local policeman had visited the wife she had said to him as he left, 'I am not suspicioned? I have not done anything wrong.' Which he thought was rather odd, particularly since he had not told her about the anonymous letter.

The next step was to inquire after the neighbour's dog which had indeed died of severe muscular contractions. It was disinterred from the garden, the Coroner halted the funeral, and both sets of organs were sent for analysis. Strychnine was identified in both instances and the Yard was called in.

They sent Chief Inspector Hugh Young, the tall, lean Scot who, as a sergeant had worked on the Messiter case in Southampton. By now, he had 24 year's-service. He soon began to learn about the stormy marriage of Mr and Mrs Major which had come to such a point that Arthur had arranged to put a notice in the local newspaper disclaiming responsibility for his wife's debts which, though not large, were many and with local tradesmen. Much of the money so saved had been spent on clothes and shoes – she had twenty pairs of high quality – an amazing number for the times and their station in life.

It turned out that Mrs Major was a cantankerous woman – bossy and boastful – always complaining about her husband, accusing him of being a drunkard and idler and of having affairs. She even suggested that *he* had been trying to poison *her*. He had 'put something in her tea'. She showed Young letters she had found addressed to him. One beginning 'to my dearest sweetheart' written by the woman next door. All of which had Young wondering why someone trying to conduct an extramarital affair should be so careless with the correspondence.

Another anonymous letter had arrived nearer the time of his death this one addressed to the Chief Constable and accusing Arthur Major of 'allways' being drunk in charge and a danger to the 'peopel' of the village. Asked to write the words she spelled them the same way.

On the day of Arthur's death, *The Horncastle News* received a letter cancelling the notice regarding her debts. The net was closing but more evidence was required. From *where* had she got the strychnine which was not as easy to acquire as arsenic. She seemed anxious that they believe that it was the corned beef he had eaten which had killed him and keen that they believed *he* had bought that himself although the son claimed *she* had sent *him* out to buy it. 'It was quite black,' she said. 'I thought at the time it was bad.'

But from where had *this* housewife got *this* poison? Like cyanide, the sale of substances containing strychnine was controlled, but was likely to be purchased by people such as gamekeepers for killing vermin which, as it turned out, was her father's occupation. He admitted to having some but he insisted that the trunk in which he kept it had only one key which he kept with him at all times and he appeared to be telling the truth.[5]

Young learned that things had got so bad with the couple that she and her son had been spending much of their time staying with her father. Young asked her if she knew about the poison and she assured him that she didn't know where he kept it and was not aware that her husband had died of strychnine poisoning.

'I never mentioned strychnine,' said Young. 'How do you know your husband died of strychnine poisoning?'

Unfazed, she claimed that was just a mistake, and started going on about the corned beef being quite black. Then she noticed that the Chief Inspector was looking tired and offered to make him a cup of tea. An offer he declined.

Eventually, a small key was found in a purse belonging to Ethel Major. Her father admitted that years ago he *had* had another key but had lost it. Now it was found. Ethel Major was charged and found Guilty. The Recommendation to Mercy was not acted upon and she was executed.[6]

One source offers some explanation for Ethel Major's strange behaviour explaining that, before her marriage, she had given birth to an illegitimate daughter which had been covered up by her parents. After a few years of marriage, Arthur Major had discovered the truth and he was furious that she refused to identify the father. From then, the marriage began to break down due to constant quarrels and his violent behaviour.[7]

It was old-fashioned arsenic which was used by the next unhappy wife: Illiterate 33-year-old Irishwoman Charlotte Bryant, who lived in Sherborne in Dorset. The couple had met when he was a soldier during The Troubles in Londonderry but back in England his services were no longer needed and they were now living in poverty on a Dorset farm. Charlotte has been described variously as a slut and a slovenly woman who neglected her children and husband in pursuit of extra-marital affairs and that she had formed a strong attachment for their lodger, Leonard Parsons, who was of gypsy stock.

From May 1935 husband Frederick suffered several bouts of severe intestinal pain and sickness, diagnosed as gastro-enteritis. On 22 December, these culminated in his death. Four grains of arsenic had been found in his body and Charlotte made the unwise comment that no-one could accuse *her* of poisoning him[8]. Detective Chief Inspector Alec Bell and Detective Sergeant Albert Tapsell were sent down from The Yard.

Given its widespread use in various substances such as weed killer and sheep dips the regulations for their purchase were even stricter. One declared that if it were colourless it must be mixed with soot but if that made it unusable it may be sold in quantities of not less than 10lbs which, I suppose made it unlikely to be bought in small quantities for domestic poisoners! Also, that the purchaser must be someone of a mature age. Nonetheless said poisoners seemed to get through.[9]

Charlotte denied any knowledge of weed killer containing arsenic so Bell bought three new paint brushes to sweep the dust from every cupboard and shelf in their cottage and analysis of the results at the new Yard laboratory revealed the poison's presence. It was proved that Charlotte had bought weed killer containing the poison, the empty tin being found in a rubbish tip at the back of their cottage. She was found Guilty and it was said that she went to her death bravely. It was also revealed that the money she had earned with her amorous affairs had helped alleviate the couple's poverty. Appeal judges refused to admit some additional evidence on the grounds that it should have been produced at the trial. It was pointed out to the Home Secretary that the prosecution had been carried out by a heavy battery of leading counsel which might have considerably affected 'the minds of a rustic jury' whilst the defence had been in the hands of a junior counsel only. But this idea was dismissed.[10]

NOTES FOR CHAPTER 18

1. In *Bloody Murder, p123,* Julian Symons pointed out that during the Thirties the style of the detective, and particularly the amateur detective changed . . . the detectives springing from the new talents of Margery Allingham, Ngaio Marsh, Nicolas Blake and Michael Innes behaved more like normal human beings and were capable of making mistakes.

Michael Gilbert observed (in *Whodunnit*, p47), that when detective story writers started to shy away from the talented amateur who solved problems by the application of intellect alone it was inevitable they should turn to the police story. 'They knew that murderers in real life were caught by policemen. They suspected – and a little research soon proved – that policemen did not catch murderers by taking thought. They caught them by taking statements.'

2. Agatha Christie: An Autobiography, p261

3. Notes for the Guidance of Coroners Officers, p8, p43 & p100

4. Calling Scotland Yard, p58

5. *Notes for the Guidance of Coroner's Officers, p8, p100, 101 & 103*

6. *The Murder Squad,* p107

7. *The Murderer's Whose Who, p217*

8. *The Murders of the Black Museum,* p338.

9. *Notes for the Guidance of Coroner's Officers, p8, p100 & p103*

10. *The Murders of the Black Museum, p339.*

Field Marshal Sir Henry Wilson, who was shot dead on his own doorstep on returning from unveiling a war memorial by two soldiers who were, like him, veterans of The Great War. *Mary Evans Picture Library*

The Illustrated London News, 12 October 1925, reported that Special Branch had made a concerted effort to restrain the Communist Part of Great Britain, culminating in a raid of its headquarters, seizing three tons of literature and arresting the entire non-executive for sedition. In court, supporters sang The Red Flag. *Mary Evans Picture Library*

Detective Superintendent Robert Honey Fabian, who captured 'The Man With a Thousand Faces' and was instrumental in bringing Scotland Yard to British and US television screens. *Courtesy of Dick Kirby*

THE READING SHOP MURDER. SPECIAL SKETCHES

The Illustrated Police News, December 10, 1925, The Reading Shop Murder Special Sketches. *With thanks to the British Newspaper Archive*

THE RECOGNITION OF A HERO! A STUDY OF A BRITISH CROWD IN 1929!

The Sketch Philip Yale Drew, the American cowboy film star being mobbed by supporters after the coroner's verdict appeared to clear him of suspicion of committing the Reading shop murder. (Drew is in the centre, facing right, with a mop of dark hair and a pale coat. *Mary Evans Picture Library*

Chief Inspector Berrett was the only bearded male in the CID. He was said to have a 'gentleman farmer look' and 'a great deal of personality.' He and Sergeant Harris were to make a formidable team handling the Reading murder. *Metropolitan Police*

Divisional Detective Inspector Charles E Leach was an authority on the methods of con men such as Rabbit, Little Ernie, The Baron, Dictionary Harry, Dave the Liar and Chicago Solly who flooded into postwar London. See his book 'On Top of the Underworld' published by Sampson Law. *Metropolitan Police*

Chief Inspector (later Superintendent) Walter Hambrook led the launch of the Flying Squad and intermittently later. His murder cases include the rejected one-legged man; London Zoo elephant trainers; and Sidney Fox, who killed his mother. *Metropolitan Police*

Frederick Porter Wensley was a Somerset gardener who rose to become a Chief Constable of Scotland Yard CID. He was of the opinion that criminals would only cease crime when they were sure they would get caught.

The Metropolitan Police Anthropometric Identification System, as adapted from French Bertillonage during the 1890s, which the Met's rapid advances in simpler fingerprint classification were soon to replace. *Metropolitan Police*

Patrick Mahon murdered Emily Kaye in a bungalow at The Crumbles in Eastbourne – an unlovely spot with which Scotland Yard detectives and pathologist Bernard Spilsbury were to become all too familiar. *Metropolitan Police*

19

A Question of Footprints

That the British Police lagged behind some other advanced countries as regards the new forensic sciences was true, particularly of England and Wales, and was one of the many matters for which they were criticised but it was largely our medical and scientific agencies which were dragging their feet, not the police.

The first European laboratory concerned *solely* with forensic science is believed to be that of the University of Lausanne in 1902. Soon after this it became the Lausanne Institute of Police Science. A forensic laboratory opened in Dresden in 1915 and another in Vienna in 1923. Sweden, Finland and Holland followed before 1925. The Los Angeles forensic Science Laboratory opened in 1923 and the FBI's in 1932[1]. In some other countries the science, which pulls together various fields such as physics, chemistry and biology, was known as Criminalistics or Police Science and forensics were dubbed 'the silent evidence'.

In the UK we turned to various specialists as needed. Spilsbury for pathology; Robert Churchill for ballistics, Alfred Swaine Taylor for poisons and so on. With his involvement in real life cases and even via his fiction Arthur Conan Doyle became credited with being highly instrumental in drawing attention to the latest forensic sciences but, in some cases, his influence was over-stated.

When comparing the advantages of crime fiction compared to real-life crime HRF Keating cited 'fiction facts' which could powerfully aid a story – as in Sherlock Holmes tales. For instance that it is possible to tell in which direction a bicycle has been ridden by the overlapping of the tyre marks – when in fact that is probably not true.[2]

However, as Professor B J Rahn points out in *The Real World of Sherlock* that 'although Conan Doyle kept abreast of the latest developments in forensic science, he only mentions fingerprinting in seven stories, and then it is 'more honoured in the breach than in observance.' In other words, Holmes notices prints 'but does not attempt to derive leads from any of them'.

In *The Boscombe Valley Mystery* (1891), as noted by Professor Rahn, footprints receive more attention. Holmes is able to derive three personal portraits (victim, his son, and assailant) plus the latter's physical description and also reconstruct movements from them – even after Lestrade has allowed the crime scene to have been trampled.[3]

In a *Study in Scarlet* (1887) Sherlock Holmes states, 'There is no branch of the detective science which is so important and so much neglected as the art of tracing footsteps' and he produces his monograph on the subject citing the use of plaster of Paris as 'a preserver of impresses'.

In fact, *way back in 1786*, a young Scottish constable solved the murder of a young girl by making a plaster cast of the bootwear at the scene of the crime and comparing these impressions against the boots of those attending her funeral.[4]

In 1839, while investigating the murder of an old women named Elizabeth Longfoot, Bow Street Runner Henry Goddard noticed that one of the three different sized footmarks leaving the scene one was 'much above ordinary size and I may say, unusually long.' Which led him to a man of bad character with large feet who turned out to be one of the suspects.[5]

In 1850, during the investigation of the murder of the Reverend Hollest 'naked footprints' were found in the parsonage grounds – one with a trace of blood which tied up with the cut on the foot of one of the accused[6] and in 1860, whilst investigating Mrs Emsley's murder, D I Thornton removed part of the floorboard which had a footprint on it to be taken to court (just as Charles Meymott Tidy was later to advocate in *Legal Medicine* in 1882). The jury could then compare the print with the boot which the suspect had been seen to throw away.[7] During *that* case, Judge Baron Pollock remarked on how *often* casts of footprints were brought into court while advising that they had to 'fit the shoe like a seal' and Major Arthur Griffiths, in his Mysteries *of Police and Crime 1, p5 (1898),* alluded *to* the *constant* use of footprints in evidence.

Later, Poirot demonstrated how to deal with footprints without losing face by dismissing them as inferior to the use of little grey cells and claiming that he wasn't going to make himself look ridiculous by lying down on the possibly damp grass to study hypothetical footprints then later claiming that the footmarks were the most important and interesting thing in the case[8].

Their *absence* at a crime scene was even noted, as in the murder of James De la Rue in 1845, when it was recorded that the ground had been 'too hard to register signs of a struggle or the footprints of the murderer'[9].

It may be correct that there was no *official* protocol for making use of them as evidence, merely common sense practise which could be improved upon.

And criminals were well aware of the evidential value of footprints – one burglar never went to work without his stick onto which a shoe (not of his size) was attached so as to leave a misleading imprint behind – the stick is still to be found in the Yard's Black Museum. And later, Harry Edward Vickers, AKA Flannelfoot, burgled his way around London, first in 1911, then during the Twenties and Thirties, by wrapping his hands and feet in rags or cloth stolen from the houses he had burgled. (One reported intention was 'to muffle his footsteps' but clearly preventing the recording of his fingerprints and footprints was equally, if not more, important.) Eventually arrested in December 1937. He was given five years penal servitude for housebreaking after 34 other offences were taken into consideration.[10]

In 1933, a committee on detective work recommended the establishment of regional laboratories. Trenchard took up the idea on behalf of the Metropolitan Police, writing to the Home Secretary suggesting the establishment of a Laboratory at the new Hendon Police College. This was opened in 1935 and, by the end of 1937, had dealt with 620 cases approximately half from the Metropolitan Police. Some civil cases were also included.[11]

Improvements were also being made in methods of acquiring information from the public which, with more police cars being equipped with wireless, could quickly be passed on to them and, in 1932, they were invited to phone in via the number Whitehall 12 12. Eventually this proved too ponderous and not direct enough and, in 1937, 999 was introduced for use in emergencies only. On the first day of operation the Information Room was overwhelmed with calls and persuading people exactly what constituted an emergency took a long time but eventually the system proved very successful judging by the increase in arrests by the crews of the wireless cars.[12]

And, of course, Scotland Yard did not rely entirely on fingerprints, photography and forensics for identification. They had a Criminal Record Office packed with the physical details and the habits of criminals; their aliases, friends, favourite taverns, personal peculiarities and methods of operation. Criminals, often being lazy, were creatures of habit, therefore the indexes were particularly useful in catching *them* but one young detective constable, Robert Fabian, found that one M.O. was a great puzzle.

Following five successful years in the CID and having now passed his sergeants exam he had been seconded to a filing and cross-indexing job in the Criminal Record Office and was feeling bored and a little resentful when he came across a curious crime popping up every few days in various far flung parts of the country – Yorkshire, Suffolk, Staffordshire, Isle of Wight. A man, carrying two heavy suitcases, would book into a good class boarding house paying a few days rent in advance. Then, he would rob all the other guests and depart, leaving several full bottles of beer behind. The total worth of the items he stole was often quite staggering. People in good class boarding houses often carried their personal treasures with them.

He left no fingerprints but, most curiously, was always

described physically and characteristically quite differently. One time he was a middle-aged Irishman with a walrus moustache; another a fair haired young art student with an effeminate manner; then an elderly man with a stammer and thick spectacles. Was there a gang? Clearly, the beer bottles had been used as ballast in his suitcase to make him appear to be a genuine traveller and were left behind to provide space for the items he had stolen.

The reports kept coming in and the young detective began keeping the details in his private notebook.[13]

Fast forward nearly a year and Robert Fabian, is now a sergeant in the Marylebone Lane CID answering a phone call from a local boarding House keeper whose residents had been robbed by 'such a nice gentleman'. The man had told her he was a lecturer at the London School of Economics and he looked the part too, with long, untidy, black hair; wing collar, black tie and pince-nez spectacles on a black silk ribbon. Oh, and with two missing front teeth . . . 'Funny you should say that – yes – he did bring with him two suitcases and left behind bottles of beer.'

Fortunately, one of the bottles retained a trace of a rubber stamp which Fabian managed to decipher and to identify the public house from which it came. Yes, agreed the landlord of that pub, there *is* a man who always buys three quarts of beer nearly every night. Doesn't drink beer himself – he only has only gin and dubonnet. 'He's a repertory actor, you see, and his friends go up to his flat for play rehearsals.'

His name was David St Bude, and, as luck would have it, he was attending a party that very night in an upstairs room. An introduction was arranged with the fair-haired young man resplendent in a light camel hair coat, brown suede shoes, butter-coloured shirt and brown velvet bow tie. When approached, despite the giveaway excitement of the other guests, he took the matter coolly, quite certain that the victims would *never* identify him, 'as the man you appear to be seeking'. Fabian assured him that with the items of disguise found in his flat it would all be up and it was.

The person whom Fabian had come to nickname 'the man with the thousand faces' received no less than five years penal servitude for the over a hundred robberies which were taken into account.[14]

Of course, the Criminal Records were *most* useful for identifying habitual criminals but not so much for murders as these are frequently one-offs. Nonetheless, in 1939, when the sister of a murdered night club singer known as The Black Butterfly who had seen her talking to a man with a cleft palette she was able to pick out his photograph from others suffering from a similar infirmity from Criminal Record Office File 410 which (the, by then) *Inspector* Fabian brought to her. He was Jim Mahoney and was proved Guilty of the singer's murder and sentenced to death but reprieved to be sent to Broadmoor Lunatic Asylum where he died the following year.[15]

The body lying in the grass beside a lane on the Southern outskirts of St Albans, Hertfordshire, was clearly out of place. Not so much due to his very heavy build but to his flashy clothes, pointed polished shoes and manicured hands. Then there was the six bullet holes in his chest, back and side and the battering his scarred face seemed to have received. Not the sort of person you usually saw in the peaceful Home Counties town known for its splendid cathedral and Roman ruins. Hertfordshire Police called in the Yard who sent the very tough, Welsh ex coal miner, Chief Inspector Frederick 'Nutty' Dew Sharpe. Also DI Cherrill and Sergeant Tasker. Since London was no distance they were soon on the scene.

The victim's pockets were empty which made robbery a possibility. There were no tyre marks or footprints in the mud and the only hint of his identity was a heavy gold signet ring with a W or M in blue enamel, a key ring engraved with some words in French and A W sewn in red cotton on his reddish grey combinations and A L on his socks, collar and shirt.

Information came in that the previous evening two men, one wearing a leather coat and cap, and a heavily powdered and rouged woman wearing a leopard skin coat, had called in to the nearby Spot Café as it was closing and insisted on being served coffee. The proprietor thought that one of the two men, who had been drinking, sounded like he might be the dead man and, after seeing the corpse, he still thought so.

Some footprints in the mud outside the café had a pattern of small circles similar to those on the soles of the victim's shoes so the Yard men sent for some plaster of Paris to take casts and dismantled an amusement machine on which the trio had played, plus the coins they had used, to take away for fingerprints. The assumption that the victim could have been shot when in the area was encouraged by the fact that a nurse living nearby reported having heard a shot. But no spent bullets were found, apart from those recovered by Spilsbury from the corpse, and the shoes he was wearing proved too big to match the footprints outside the cafe. Many women owning leopard skin coats were identified, including the customer who had been in the Spot Café, but to no effect. Dead End. Clearly, information was needed from the public.

The aid of the Press was sought but, as appealingly mysterious as was the case, extremely strong competition was coming from the other current very big news story – the death of King George V. He had died a week earlier, on 20, January, 1936, and the newspapers were now awash with pictures of the vast crowds queuing to witness his lying-in-state and of the many Heads of State and Royalty arriving at Victoria Station and Croydon Airport. And even, (in the pages of the *Daily Herald)* of Mr Litvinov who would be representing Soviet Russia.

Nonetheless, the *Dumped Body Murder*[16], did make it to compete with all the Royal stories in the Press. And, by now, information from the underworld had begun filtering through telling of a tremendous fight in a Soho flat where a prostitute had taken a client who attacked her and her ponce had come to the rescue. Nutty Sharpe had already decided that this was probably a London murder and, eventually, a man recognised the description of the victim as that of Emile Allard 'a dealer in cheap jewellery' who lived in James Street, off Oxford Street. It turned out Allard was much more than that.

Sharpe and his men combed Soho's dens and prostitute's flats while the dead man's fingerprints revealed that Emile Allard was, in fact, a Latvian or was he a French Canadian? known as Red Max Kassel, and although he had no police record in Britain, he was well involved with the white slave traffic worldwide. The steady stream of information and rumour eventually caused the truth to be revealed. The name of Pierre Henri Alexandre kept coming up and *he* did admit that he *knew* a man named Max the Red, who 'ran a number of women'. (At that time London was awash with foreigners who brought in prostitutes and married them to British men so they could not be deported.) Alexandre was also one of these but he wasn't telling Sharpe anything else.

However, a French prostitute operating from one of Alexandre's flats in Soho and Inspector Benson of Vine Street police station, had heard that, on 23 January, there had been a row and a smashing of glass there. The flat was now deserted but they broke in to find three recently-renewed window-panes; whips, torture instruments and a pile of obscene pictures – all the typical prostitutes aids. Also, in the living room a curtain which had been neatly shortened with a pair of scissors, and minute spots on the bathroom floor which turned out to be blood and, tucked away, the Ministry of Health Insurance card of the prostitute's maid, Marcelle Aubin.

When traced, Marcelle insisted she knew *nothing* about Emil Allard and that it was *she* who had broken the windows when she slipped and fell against them. By now the prostitute, Suzanne Naylor, was in Paris because her mother was ill, and so it seemed, was her ponce, George Lacroix.

Alexandre was still not talking so Sharpe seized his car and, when bloodstains were found on the back seat, the pressure grew. He decided to come clean, as did the maid. On the night on 23 January George Lacroix had asked Kassel, who owed him some money, to come to the flat. Kassel had still refused to pay him back and had insulted him again. There had been a quarrel, then there were shots. It was the injured Kassell who had deliberately broken the windows while shouting for help and trying to get air. He had been begging to be taken to hospital insisting he would lie about who had shot him. Then, at last, he died. The prostitute Suzanne and her maid cleaned up the mess. Alexandre (who actually owned the flat) was sent for and the body was taken to be deposited somewhere out in the sticks.

So, in the end, the case had been solved by information, local knowledge, hard work, forensics and some official force – the elements of real detection.

Officers were sent to Paris to retrieve Naylor and Lacroix but there were problems over extradition and the case was eventually heard in Paris where Lacroix pleaded self defence and was sentenced to ten years with hard labour. Suzanne Naylor was acquitted and the drama was over[17] although the racket of importing foreign prostitutes and living off them continued for many years even until I served in the West End in the 1950s and was obliged to pose as a prostitute to test whether the new law, The Street Offences Act, 1959, designed to regain control of the streets, would actually work.[18]

NOTES FOR CHAPTER NINETEEN

1. *Murder Under the Microscope,* p48-49
2. *Whodunnit,* p12
3. *The Real World of Sherlock* p155-6
4. Dwane S Hilderbrand CLPE; Iowa Division of the International Association for Identification Conference. 4 November, 2020.
5. *Memoirs of a Bow Street Runner,* p145
6. *Truly Criminal: A Crime of Consequence,* p198
7. *Dreadful Deeds and Awful Murders,* p149

8. *Murder on the Links,* p25 and p85

9. *Scotland Yard's First Cases,* p79

10. *Wikipedia:* Harry Edward Vickers *(Flannelfoot)*

11. *The Official Encyclopedia of Scotland Yard,* p94-5

12. *Ibid,* p285-6

13. *Fabian of the Yard,* p196-198

14. *Ibid,* p198-203

15. *Ibid,* p190-195

16. *Daily Herald,* 27 January, 1936

17. *Murder Squad,* P117-129

18. *Lady Policeman,* p19

20

Gaudy Night

'*Gaudy Night* so powerfully reflects Sayers' belief in equality between the sexes that the book is often called the first major feminist mystery novel' writes Martin Edwards, while pointing out that the book, published in 1935, was not unanimously approved of and that Julian Symons dismissed it as a 'woman's novel'. However, her 'unrelenting focus on female independence influenced many other women novelists' which Martin thought was a legacy 'of which any writer could be proud'.[1]

A 'gaudy' is an Oxford University feast which acts as a reunion for the alumni and Harriet Vane is invited to one at Shrewsbury College and later, the Dean contacts her asking for help to solve an outbreak of vandalism and of anonymous letters.

There are no murders in the book. Harriet requests Wimsey's help and, at the end she finally accepts his proposal of marriage. But central to the plot is a woman's right to an academic education and Sayers regarded it as the pinnacle of her achievement as a novelist.[2]

She was falling out of love with detective novels and, after the next one – *Busman's Honeymoon* – which had started out as a play,[3] she wrote no more.

Agatha Christie, however, was giving her readers two or three books a year and, whilst accompanying her husband Max on his archaeological excavations in the Middle East, was able to offer the depression-worn readers a touch of the exotic with titles such as *Murder in Mesopotamia* (1936), *and Death on the Nile* (1937) plus the landmark, *ABC Murders* (1936), in which the victim's initials are the same as that of the crime scene.

A hint of travel excitement came too from Freeman Wills Crofts with *The 12.30 From Croydon,* which gives us a body on the 12.30 flight from Croydon to Paris and, in flashback, we live with the killer at every stage. *The Illustrated London News* dismisses it as 'a standard Freeman Wills Crofts, a well thought out mystery, but too amply padded and ponderous'.

The Literary Lounger in *The Sketch* was much kinder and clearly didn't see Crofts as a humdrum. Indeed, he gives a long, well considered, review of this inverted, anti-capitalist, novel. He had seldom read a better trial scene in any novel but was sorry to see so little of Inspector French. 'This most amiable and modest of detectives remained behind the scenes nearly all the time.' But the case had gained him promotion, 'and he well deserved it.'

In 1937, came two more Scotland Yard films. From the U.S.: *Blake of Scotland Yard.* Oddly, the latter was an edited version of a serial film of the same name which had been playing in our cinemas for a number of years. The police characters were Chief Inspector Henderson and Mimi (a policewoman posing as a dancer).

The Blake of the title was Sir James Blake 'a leading figure in crime fighting' who had retired from the Yard so that he could assist his niece and her friend develop an apparatus which they hoped would prevent wars but which was stolen by a gang of criminals led by the elusive *Scorpion*. Quite upmarket this one, judging by the caste list, which included a butler, a Baron and a Count. But this could be misleading given that a 'Duchess' turns out to be a Gang Moll and another actor plays the 'lead thug'.[4]

The other film, *Wanted by Scotland Yard,* was out of a British studio, and the characters appeared to be from lower down the Class chain but it was rather more romantic. A criminal attempting to go straight to please his girlfriend recognises Standish, a man he is about to rob, as the man who killed his previous girlfriend, and his motivations change. The Yard men involved are Inspector Williams and a character known as 'Sherlock'[5].

The day-to-day crime occupying the real detectives at the lower end of the scale included a rash of pickpockets, shoplifters and burglars. Also, pursuit of jewellery thieves who stole from actresses backstage, aristocracy who were taking part in glittering affairs and, from the actual jewellers, either by smash and grab or by the managers or assistants becoming in thrall to some convincing shopper who walked off with the goods.

Another really big remaining problem, were the Race Track Gangs who had been causing mayhem at the race tracks ever since the end of the war. Little security was provided by the track organisers and not only were there many crooked bookmakers who tended to welsh when the favourite won but there were the various regional gangs who indulged in all kinds of crimes. Among the worst of these were (from London): *The Bethnal Green Mob*, the *Hoxton Gang* and the *Italian Mob* and, (from the Provinces): the *Leeds Crowd* and their allies, the *Birmingham Boys*.

They not only demanded protection money from the bookmakers but bullied and tricked patrons and had vicious fights for supremacy with each other. The newly-formed Flying Squad took them on in 1921 and had had an early success with the problem after the Birmingham Boys had mistakenly attacked the Leeds mob on their way home thinking they were the Italian Mob. A horrendous battle ensued until someone shouted 'We're the Leeds Crowd!' and the Birmingham Boys ran to their charabanc.

On the way home from track duties Sergeant Dawson happened upon the Birmingham Boys in a public house and arrested all 28 who immediately made to rush him. But his Superintendent had taken the unusual step of arming him and he threatened to shoot the first man who tried to escape. They were given prison terms of nine months to three years.

But the battles continued nonetheless. From 1927 on the Flying Squad's chief weapon was Nutty Sharpe, made strong by his four years working down the mines and playing rugby for a police team and the fact that he was also immensely brave. He frequently faced them down, sometimes even pretending to be a staggering drunk to entice muggers to attack him.

The Flying Squad's final victory came in June, 1936. Information was received that a member of the Hoxton Mob had been attacked by the Sabinis and that a raiding party was to be sent to the Lewes racetrack to extract revenge. Sharpe led a strong contingent to Lewes where they found a bookmaker and his clerk, associates of the Sabinis, had been attacked by thirty of the Hoxton Gang with hatchets, hammers, knuckledusters and crowbars, and they had received terrible injuries. The Squad arrested most of them but, incredibly they were released on bail and were able to threaten the victims if they gave evidence. But, bravely, they did, and at last suitable sentences were awarded. Two received five years penal servitude, eleven others two, three or four years. The effect of these sentences on the number of arrests necessary after that was dramatic.[6]

At the other end of the scale or at least not obviously violent were the aforementioned Poison Pen Letter writers who seemed to be taken rather seriously. During Inspector Henry's service there appeared to be something of an epidemic. He claimed to have handled, or assisted in, many such cases among the upper classes, professionals, and even 'in the mean streets of backyard land'.

He insisted that they caused more misery than blackmailers and that the affects on the recipients might 'not infrequently' be suicide, divorce or a nervous breakdown. He believed the writers were almost all women. Many of them 'well reared creatures, who have led secluded lives and are repressed'. So serious was this 'menace' wrote D I Henry, in his autobiography, that Superintendent Thomson, an officer expert in its detection, had been put in charge of a Poison-Pen Squad!

The letters might be from rejected lovers, dismissed employees or just women with nothing better to do and clearly the CID spent a surprising amount of time tracking them down. As in the case of Sir Austen Chamberlain and his friend Sir Warden Chillcott, M.P. who both were regularly receiving scurrilous letters. With the help of the Post Office, D I Henry and his sergeant made many enquiries and a likely suspect was shadowed for weeks. She was a good-looking woman about 25 years-old, who emerged from a big house in a well-to-do area. Finally, she was stopped, a letter found on her and she was arrested.

She turned out to be the daughter of a prominent public man and 'as might be expected, she was not in good mental health'. He does not reveal what happened to her next or what the letters actually said.

In another instance, they went as far as having a female detective take a job as a maid in the house of a suspect who was 'a very highly connected woman'. And, when a very highly connected professional man received letters accusing him of having an association with one of his staff, D.I. Henry had a chat with the man's wife broadly hinting that he had discovered their authorship – after which the letters ceased.

Actresses frequently received such letters many of them from people 'with warped minds and foul tongues'. So, it seems, trolls are nothing new. However, the only letter threatening to *kill* the recipient (a woman) was from a man. He was traced, found to be 'mental' and sent to an appropriate home.[7]

Of course, one might imagine it would be best to keep quiet about such missives but one actress clearly didn't think so judging by an item in a newspaper announcing: '**THREATENED** – CALLED IN 'YARD'. *Rene Ray, the film actress, has told Scotland Yard about a threatening letter. The writer – Miss Ray thinks he is a religious maniac – declared he would tear from her throat the cross she wore in the film, The Rat.*' A photo of Miss Ray avec the cross was appended.[8]

Another poison pen recipient who made the news was

12-year-old Prince Rainier, son of Prince Pierre of Monaco, who was attending school in England. Apparently the boy had been telling Scotland Yard about receiving anonymous letters and it came into the news when Special Branch men stopped him boarding a boat for a holiday at home and insisted on taking him under their protection.[9] It turned out this was all about a custody battle over the boy who grew up to become the ruler of Monaco and to save Monte Carlo from the decay into which it had apparently fallen.

Of course, all this evil letter writing did not escape the attention of our doughty detective novelists. As we have noted, anonymous letters were a problem in *Gaudy Night* and, leading one of Agatha Christie's lists of notes on ideas for short stories, were the words 'Poison Pen'[10] though it was to be 1942 before one of her detective novels, *The Moving Finger,* centred on the subject.

In the case of *The Moving Finger* D I Henry's opinions on the affects of such letters were justified in that they *resulted* in two murders and an attempted murder and, it being a Christie novel, suspicions moved from one character to another. 'Inspector Graves: an expert on poison pen letters from Scotland Yard' was called in, but it was neither he nor even Miss Marple who solved the case. This was left to Jerry Burton, a pilot still recuperating after a plane crash followed by long stints in hospitals.

The Moving Finger turned out to be one of the author's favourites and it was later one of those adapted for television and radio.

And there were still quite a lot of guns around. Their

lingering presence was revealed amongst the smaller news items such as '*Man Found Shot in London Flat*', '*Man Found Shot and Burned*' and *Family Wiped Out on* Holiday'. This last was about a man deciding to depart this world and take all his family with him including a four and a five-year-old child.

Guns were also still being used in detective novels such as Christie's *The Murder at the Vicarage* in which the unpleasant Colonel Protheroe is found shot dead in the Vicar's study and when confessing a (not guilty) character throws down a Mauser 25; and in *The Second Gong* in which the bullet goes through the dinner gong confusing characters into wondering whether the second gong for dinner had gone or not. Also in the short story, *The Man Who Knew,* in which Harley Street Specialist had been shot through the heart and his money-stretched-but-innocent heir is left holding the pistol. This was something of a locked room mystery, and later became *The Red Signal.* But Agatha *may* have been thinking twice about guns when, amongst her notes for *Lord Edgeware Dies* she is deciding about getting rid of the Secretary who has seen too much, she writes 'Shoot? Or Stab?' then crosses out the 'Shoot?'[11]

However, reality was still providing attention-grabbing shooting incidents such as the attempt to assassinate the King, Edward VIII, at the Trooping of the Colour on 16 July, 1936.

The revolver in this case was brand new and found to be loaded and cocked but the man who aimed it, George Andrew McMahon, claimed he had been hired for £150 by a foreign power to kill the King but it seems, since he had never fired a gun before, they must have been a rather inefficient foreign power. And it turned out that when examined the gun was not accurate beyond ten yards and the King, on horseback, was more than twice that distance away and a moving target.

The potential assassin had been carrying it wrapped in newspaper and as he drew it out an observant Special Constable knocked it from his hand and, according to McMahon, it skidded across the road frightening the horses.[12] His objective tended to alter and the incident, originally claimed to be an assassination attempt, was eventually rather played down as demonstrated by the *Somerset County Herald* on the 1st of August:

McMAHON FOR TRIAL
ROYAL PROCESSION INCIDENT
'DID NOT INTEND TO HARM THE KING'

And McMahon was soon claiming that he had been intending to kill *himself* but had changed his mind and threw the gun towards the King to get his attention. He had recently sent the King a petition re a false imprisonment charge and was sure that, if the King knew about it, he would *do* something. (Clearly he was taken in by Edward's recent 'Something must be done' when faced with poverty-stricken Welsh miners.) However, McMahon was neither a marksman nor a madman, claimed Gordon Honeycomb in his *Murders of the Black Museum,* just 'a publicity-seeking fantasist.' He was convicted of 'producing a revolver near the person of the King with intent to alarm His Majesty' and sentenced to twelve months hard labour[13].

Although the British were said to have been kept uninformed about the King's affair with Mrs Simpson it does seem that there *were* hints such as this little insert in *The Western Mail and*

South Wales News on Tuesday 4th August, 1936. It was slotted into a column describing the Prime Minister's simple holiday in a mansion in Wales where he won a Gold Medal at a Flower Show and collected a prize of 15 shillings.

THE KING'S HOLIDAY
From our Own Correspondent
Marseillies, Monday

I learn on excellent authority that the King will travel overland to Venice, where he will join the yacht Nahlin for his Mediterranean cruise.

It was the presence of Mrs Simpson on this cruise which was said to have alerted the World – but not the U.K. -- about their affair. But matters were speeding on and by December, 1936, the King was making his goodbye speech to the Nation.

All this affected one Detection Club member, Anthony Berkeley, so much that he became obsessed with the idea of halting the marriage because he imagined, as did many others, that Edward was the man for the job. Berkeley spent much time and money cooking up a case against the King and Wallace to prove they had committed adultery – which he hoped would compromise her divorce proceedings -- and so prevent her marriage to the King. *This,* and his other obsessions, began to weary fellow members and affect Berkeley's health and work flow. Fortunately, his efforts failed, and we were given a more suitable King.

Berkeley rallied and his next crime novel, *Trial and Error,* turned out to be 'a masterpiece of wit and ingenuity'.[14]

NOTES FOR CHAPTER 20

1. *The Golden Age of Murder,* p277-8
2. *Ibid*
3. *Ibid,* p307-8 and p340-42
4. Wikipedia -- *Blake of Scotland Yard* (1937 film)
5. Wikipedia – *Wanted by Scotland Yard*
6. *The Race Track Gangs, by Dick Kirby, The Peeler,* Issue 7, 2002
7. *D I Henry's Famous Cases,* p31-35
8. *Daily Herald,* 25 April, 1938
9. *Western & South Wales News,* 4 August, 1936
10. *Agatha Christies's Murder in the Making, p235*
11. Ibid, p166
12. *The Murders of the Black Museum,* p341-2
13. *Ibid*
14. *The Golden Age of Murder,* p360-1

21
Suburban Comfort

Of course murder was still rearing its ugly head but was no respecter of a senior police officer's social arrangements. On the evening of March 3rd, 1937, Divisional Detective Inspector Jack Henry was in full evening dress, about to leave for the CID Officers Annual Dinner, when he was informed that there had been 'a nasty case of burglary' in Worcester Park, Surrey. He was a man who loved all the glamour of show business and had worked for months arranging that night's cabaret, nonetheless he removed his top hat, gave instructions as to which officers and specialists would be needed at the scene, and jumped into a waiting car.

He soon found himself in the comfortable, middle class suburban home of middle-aged journalist, Walter Scott; his second wife, Sara Alice Scott, and their sixteen-year-old son Donald Walter. Four of Mr Scott's other children had grown up and left home but, until recently, another son, (Mrs Scott's stepson) 22-year-old carpenter and joiner Douglas Leoni Scott, had still been living with them.

Mrs Scott was lying on the dining room floor her head covered in blood. A scarf was tied tightly around her neck, and she was quite dead. The sixteen-year-old son had discovered her body when he returned home from school at half past four having had lunch with her only four hours earlier. He had pulled off the cloth covering her face, felt for a heartbeat, then run next door for help.

Mrs Scott's empty purses rested by her empty handbag, cabinet drawers had been rifled, a nearly empty bottle of brandy in the kitchen bore fingerprints and Mr Scotts' expensive Singer motor car was missing. Local people had seen the stepson, Douglas Leoni Scott en route to see her that afternoon and he had later been witnessed trying to force the garage door off its hinges . . Clearly, this was going to be a no brainer. Not one for our clever fictional detectives . . . No need for deep thought or flashes of brilliance.

The hue and cry to locate the stepson began. Police officers all over England and Wales were alerted (via 'the Yard's Special wireless station') to look out for five-foot-ten, Douglas Leoni Scott, who had dark, brushed-back, hair and was driving a Singer motor car, index APL . . . . .

Meanwhile, Spilsbury, fingerprint ace Cherill, and DI O'Brien from the photographic department, were all arriving at the scene. As was, Chief Constable Horwell whom we first met as a young Divisional DI attempting and succeeding in solving the Pembridge Square murder. He was now apparently much admired and established and was present at the scene 'to review the situation'.

Many sightings of the Singer car came in from far and wide. The most worthy pursuit effort came from PC Viney of the Bristol Constabulary who sighted the vehicle in the early hours and chased it until he fell from his bicycle exhausted.

Meanwhile, his fellow cop rushed to a telephone and, as a result, his Inspector set off in a police car, caught up, and arrested the wanted man.

Scott declined to answer any of D I Henry's questions insisting on writing out his own self-pitying statement. His life had been downed from the start . . . while at school, he frequently had trouble with his stepmother and this went on as he started work. Nothing ever seemed to go his way. He wanted a new start and had gone to see her to persuade her to take him back home to live as he couldn't afford to live in his lodgings any longer.

'She would not see reason in any shape and ordered me out.' When he didn't move she had made to push him 'and therefore we struggled. Whatever happened was an accident, purely. '

'P.S. In my temper, I struck her with my fist.'

More than once, it seems, since Spilsbury found the side of her face badly beaten and there was a wound on the top of her head.

However, he was ably defended by Norman Birkett, K.C. and, of course, the jury was predominately male (9 men, 3 women). The prosecution based most of their case around theft which was a bit of a mistake. It allowed Mr Birkett to say witheringly 'Murder for £2?' which apparently was all the money the stepson had found in the purses. Changing tack thus, allowed him to suggest that manslaughter would be a more suitable verdict – on the grounds of provocation. Hate of his stepmother had been suggested, 'There is nothing so bitter in all the emotions of the world as family quarrels or animosities.'

Amazingly they got their manslaughter verdict and the now 24-year-old Douglas Leoni Scott was sentenced to 10 years penal servitude.[1]

Not very far north of the Scott family in similar suburban comfort in Wimbledon lived Percy and Georgina Casserley. Fifty-eight-year-old Percy was the recently-retired Managing Director of London Brewers John Watney & Co Ltd. Once athletic, he was now an alcoholic getting through a bottle and a half of whisky a day and, unsurprisingly, he was irascible, abusive and unsociable though not violent. He had recently spent a month receiving treatment for his alcoholism and when he returned home 38-year-old Georgina had told him that she was pregnant which, considering their sexual relations had ceased some time previously, was not welcome news.

The previous year, building work been going on next door and one day the young and attractive Mrs Casserley had asked the foreman, strapping, handsome, thirty-five-year-old Edward Royal Chaplin, if he would like a cup of tea. Things developed from there on.

Percy Casserley was away again having treatment when Georgina wrote to him asking for a divorce which he refused. 'Do you think I am such a fool as to give you up for someone else?'

He had just arrived home again on 22 March, 1937.

On 23 March, 1937, D I Henry was just about to leave Putney Police Station after a hard day's work when he got the call. This time, the body on the floor of the lounge was that of a man – Percy Casserley. There were wounds to his head, a .25 cartridge case beside it and, by his leg, a live shell of a similar calibre. So far, thought Henry, it was a possible suicide – except where was the gun? He tried to see Mrs Casserley, who had discovered her husband injured but unconscious, and she had run next door for help. But she was still next door, in bed, too upset to talk.

There was no sign of forcible entry and in the dining room, a curious sight. On the floor, beside sideboard all lined up, were a silver coffee pot, coffee percolator, trophy cup, basin and teapot – a possible disturbed burglary then? But, also, a bloodstained torch broken in two. On examination, two gunshot wounds to the head of Percy Casserley were found and he had also been struck across the head with something blunt and hard – *not* suicide then. Having found a greyish bone button, with strands of thread attached, D I Henry ordered an examination of all the victim's clothes to see if such a button was missing but there was not. This was more like it. A real clue.

They learned that Percy Casserley owned an automatic pistol but it was missing. Throughout the night the house and grounds were searched for the gun without success but what they *did* find, locked in a chest of drawers in a bedroom, was a bundle of tender love letters signed 'Ted'. Henry felt that at last they were getting somewhere.

Inquiries revealed the identity of Ted and Henry found him working on a building site in Epsom.

He already knew about Mr Casserley's death and exclaimed, 'Yes, it's terrible. I read about it in the papers.' He agreed to come with them, went to a shed and came out wearing a trilby and putting on a raincoat which was wet and very stained, although it was a lovely day. And the top button was missing. Ted quickly accounted for the staining by drawing attention to a cut he had made on his hand that morning whilst doing brickwork. And when Henry compared the button he had found with those on the man's coat Chaplin promptly pulled a button from his pocket claiming *this* was the missing one although plainly the button the DI was holding was a match and his was not.

They took him to a police station where, searching him, they found another love letter. Chaplin admitted the affair but denied any knowledge of Mr Casserley's death. In Chaplin's flat they found a bloodstained life preserver (cosh) and in a bucket of rubbish a diamond ring. The blood turned out to be of the same group as Casserley's and the cosh, according to Spilsbury, could have been responsible for the three head wounds. The ring was clearly being worn by the victim on a large photograph in his room.

Later, Mrs Casserley, who had first claimed she had gone out for a walk and come back to find her injured husband on the floor, decided she now, in the presence of her solicitor, wished to tell the truth. Then she burst into tears so the solicitor took over saying to her, 'On Wednesday afternoon, your husband threatened to shoot you?'.

She nodded, 'Yes.'

'And did Mr Chaplin offer to go back to the house and see your husband?'

'Yes.'

'You went back together?'

'Yes.'

When they got there Chaplin sent her upstairs and he went in to see Percy. She heard voices raised in anger. Chaplin, too, decided to talk explaining that he had confessed to her husband that he was responsible for Mrs Casserley's condition and that Casserley had replied, 'Oh, so it's you, you swine.' (He had imagined it 'must be some tea-planter home on six month's leave from Ceylon'.) To protect Georgina, Chaplin had suggested to Casserley that she come away with him that night or he would get her police protection?

Casserley went to his desk, sat with his head in his hands, then opened a drawer and took out a pistol. Chaplin had dived forward and seized his arm forcing him to drop the gun but he managed to pick it up with his other hand and a struggle ensued during which the gun went off. Suddenly, Casserley gripped Chaplin's testicles, squeezed and would not stop so Chaplin grasped the torch lying on the desk and struck him on the head with it. Then Casserley had got the gun again and it went off again, shooting him in the head. Afterwards, Chaplin picked up the gun and the box of cartridges and took them home putting them in a drawer on top of the cosh he had bought so his ailing father could protect himself. Which was how the cosh got Casserley's blood on it.

Chaplin was charged with the murder of Percy Casserley but he was not downcast. 'All the time he came in contact with us' reported Henry, 'Chaplin was always in very jolly spirits...' 'and he liked being well dressed for his appearances in court... he seemed particularly keen that his appearance should meet the approval of the women present.'

Georgina was arrested and charged with being an accessory after the fact but bailed from Holloway Prison where it was said she had been forbidden to have a bath and made to scrub floors which her lawyer claimed was no way to treat a lady and a pregnant one at that.

The judge, Mr Justice Humphreys, while quite insultingly cutting about Mrs Casserley, whom he said some had treated as though she was some sort of heroine when she was merely 'a participator in a vulgar and sordid intrigue', reminded the jury that if they decided that Mr Casserley had been shot 'in the heat of passion in the course of a quarrel so serious that the accused lost complete control of himself' and had not intended to cause his death they might convict him of manslaughter. Which they did.

Edward Chaplin was given 12 years penal servitude, served eight, was met at the prison gates by Mrs Casserley and they went off to the Registry Office to get married.[2]

Divisional D I Henry had already gone to bed 'after a hard day's work' when the call came to take him to Wimbledon again. This time, to a little bit further West – to Somerset Road – aka 'Lovers Lane' – just off Wimbledon Common. There, he met up with the crew of a police car and John William Love of Kingston Fire Brigade who had been driving along Somerset Road when his headlights picked out a dark shape lying by the grass verge.

He had at first thought it was a tree, but then realised it was the body of a woman. She had terrible injuries to her head, bruises on her legs and tyre marks on her right instep – as if she had been the victim of a hit and run. Although she was fully dressed in a black worsted coat and skirt, she was hatless and there was no handbag to be found which gave Henry the impression that she had been killed elsewhere then brought to Somerset Road and run over. Of course this lack of a handbag was most important to him as it meant that the first vital move in a murder enquiry – establishing the victim's identity – was not possible. (We carry our identity in our bags and pockets.) Ignorance of her place of death added another difficulty – no crime scene. A lot harder this one.

Her fingerprints found no match at Scotland Yard. Nor did plaster castes of the tyre treads or scrapings of the sandy surface of the road produce any results from the police laboratory at Hendon. A search for a bloodstained motor car and/or driver at garages, coffee stalls and among the police, also turned up nothing. Nor did mass searches of nearby commons or fields. 'The best detective brains of the Yard have been brought into the investigation. Chief Constable Horwell, Superintendent Sands and Superintendent Donaldson 'of Brighton Trunk crime fame' announced the *Daily Herald* a couple of days later.

The newspaper also helped out with the physical description of the victim which had been broadcast by the BBC the previous evening. She was aged about thirty, 5ft 4ins, slim build, flat chested, weight about 7 stone, hair: darkish brown, eyebrows plucked and stencilled and fingernails polished red. The headline picked out the most outstanding element: **Stencilled Eyebrows**.

There was also news about a couple of cars which had been seen moving about the scene that night and there was a photograph of Mrs Boston, the elderly domestic servant who had noticed them out of her window thinking they were just more Lovers Lane nuisances. The cars were 'small'. One was shabby and one of the motorists was thickset and wore a dark grey hat. Mrs Boston had also seen a *van* approach, stop, then move on again. There were also several photographs of the leading detectives in their dark suits and trilby hats.

A photograph of the dead victim resulted in scores of identifications – none fruitful. The detectives were despairing. 'Scores of people came forward . . . time after time our hopes were raised, only to be dashed again,' wrote Henry in his memoirs. But, *eventually*, someone identified the victim as Rose Muriel Atkins or 'Irish Rose' or 'Pat'.

From that, they were able to trace her movements that night as, dressed in her 'somewhat distinctive costume' of a black suit, black fur with a white tip to the tail, a little white openwork hat and transparent lace gloves, she was seen to get off a bus at Parkside, Wimbledon, at 10pm and, *finally*, they discovered a young woman who had seen her alive at 11.30pm.

This young woman had begun to approach Rose, wanting to speak to her, but when a small green van had driven up, Rose had spoken to the driver, got in, and they had driven off towards Somerset Road.

Small shabby cars and men wearing in dark grey hats were forgotten as the hunt for small green vans began. Hundreds were inspected in all parts of London and throughout England. Fingerprint ace, Fred Cherrill, concentrated his magnifying glass on the tyre print on the stocking on Rose's right leg, consulted a number of tyre stockists and examined samples until he was able to say that a tyre of this size would be fitted to an Austen Seven or a Morris Minor – which narrowed things down a great deal.

However, the van eventually came to them when a wholesale boot repairers reported to Tottenham Court Road Police Station that one of their drivers, George Brain, had embezzled £32 2s.11d and absconded leaving his van with the fellow employee whom he usually dropped off home every evening. The van turned out to be a small green Morris Eight and had clearly been recently washed but retained some blood stains.

Hastening to Brain's home D I Henry found the bird had

flown but learned from his mother that George had been out until 12.30 on the night of the murder and, after telling her the van had broken down, had been uncharacteristically quiet. Searching the firm's garage bloodstained articles were discovered and, eventually, Rose Atkins handbag, empty of money.

The search for George Brain was intense. 'It was hard to conceive of there being so many men in England who looked like George Brain'. Extra staff had to man the Information Room telephones day and night to cope with the calls and more than 2000 statements were taken. Even Brain's fiancé, whom he was supposed to be marrying in a couple of days, had no idea where he was.

Police and public had been searching for eleven days when George Brain was suddenly found, accidently, by a schoolboy who knew him by sight and who was on holiday with his parents in the Thameside resort of Sheerness. Strolling along the beach he suddenly spotted Brain, bearded and tanned though he was, hiding in the cliffs above them. He told his father, who told the police, and they found him lying in some gorse bushes fifty yards down the cliff. It was an ideal hiding place claimed Henry, unfrequented by man for weeks on end and Brain had hoped to hide there until things blew over then get out of the country in a tramp ship.

He had met up with Rose three or four times, Brain admitted, but on this occasion she had demanded money from him and when he said she wouldn't get much out of him she had threatened to tell his firm about their van being out late. 'I struck her with my hand and she started screaming'. Then, as Henry noted, 'Brain resorted to the usual plea of murderers'.

Everything seemed to go blank and he hit her with his starting handle which he kept in the van. And when he 'came to' there was her body lying in the van. Apparently he had found only four shillings in her handbag – not realising that she kept her money in her fur stole – sometimes quite a lot. So, he took £30 of the firm's money, went to the dogs at Wimbledon track and lost the lot.

Throughout their acquaintance Brain was boisterous and wise-cracking. Henry did not believe his story about Rose demanding money. The blows to her head had been savage. The jury did not believe him either and convicted him in 15 minutes. A wry note: Brain was hanged for murdering a woman who 'was already in the early stages of an incurable malady'. [3]

NOTES FOR CHAPTER TWENTY-ONE

1. *Detective Inspector Henry's Famous Cases,* p145-149.
2. *Ibid,* p113-121; *Murders of the Black Museum,* p 348-358.
3. *Detective Inspector Henry's Famous Cases,* p50-58.

22

The Enemy Within

Despite all the optimistic signs to the contrary it seemed that IRA militants were still most anxious to attack the British mainland and had been carefully laying out their detailed plans of attack. American financial support was currently low due to a series of squabbles but this was judged to be a good moment with Britain weak as it appeased German aggression.

A lot of work had gone into what was known as their S Plan, new faces had been recruited which were completely unknown to The Branch, a series of bomb-making courses had been held and safe houses established on the mainland so, on the night of 28 November, 1938, they held a full scale exercise to blow up some customs posts in Northern Ireland. Alas, one of their bombs exploded prematurely killing all three of the IRA volunteers, one of whose' last words were 'stand back John James . . .there's a wee mistake'. [1]

Nonetheless, on Monday, 16 January, 1939, the IRA went ahead with seven bombs exploding on the British mainland: two in London at power stations; three in Manchester, one in Birmingham and one next to an electricity pylon near the Northumberland market town of Alnwick.

There *had* been a warning *of sorts*. Four days earlier, *The Irish Republican Army* wrote to the Foreign Secretary suggesting that the British Government should signify its intentions to evacuate and Declare Abdication from their country or else, in four days time, they would take appropriate action.

At 6am on the morning of 17 January, the Branch sprung into action, rounding up thirty-three known I.R.A. sympathisers and finding bomb making equipment, rifles and handguns. In Mornington Crescent, in Camden Town, they woke up three men asleep next to their bomb factory. Similar finds were made in Manchester and Cardiff. Then more in London.

At the address of Peter Stuart in New Oxford Street were found many copies of the IRA proclamation of the intended attack; much internal correspondence and over a thousand rubber balloons. It seemed that Stuart was a specialist in manufacturing "airships" that ignited when the acid content had eaten through the rubber and was exposed to air. When they found a ton of iron oxide and two tons of sodium chloride at another address, and at another, a copy of the IRA strategy plan, they realised that 16 January was just the beginning of the onslaught.

That same day there were two explosions aimed at disabling power stations and cutting water supplies and two failed attempts. An attempt to bomb an electricity pylon stretching across the Manchester Ship Canal failed due to a faulty timer. A porter was killed in Manchester.

In London, on Saturday, 4 February, bombs exploded in the left luggage departments of Leicester Square and Tottenham Court Road underground stations, seriously injuring two people. In Liverpool there was a failed attempt to blow in a wall of Walton Gaol and fires broke out in suburban shops and, the following day, in department stores in Coventry.

The Branch Officers decided that Peter Stuart's handwriting matched some of the signatures found on documents, therefore he was undoubtedly the 'Operations Officer, Britain'. A senior GHQ officer named Mason who, as well as giving operational instructions, also gave advice on how to avoid being spotted as a potential bomber: by not having a typical Irish accent; by not wearing a trench coat and by not keeping their hands in its pockets. Also, no green scarves nor hats worn at rakish angles. Similar advice had been issued during the Fenian attacks in the 1880s but in that instance, it was their U.S. roots they were trying to hide (American accents, 'distinctive carriage' and the cut of their trousers).

It was noticed that the S Plan was quite sophisticated and well prepared. More so than previous IRA plans, which led the Branch to believe it may have been written with German Intelligence assistance. In that, they were correct, although the Germans were to become a little impatient with the increasing number of bombs being aimed at civilian targets such as, toilets, department stores, hotels and left luggage depositories, when they would rather the IRA concentrated on military targets and, also, since they were hoping to infiltrate Britain via Ireland, too much anti Irish feeling might hinder that.

The bombs kept coming and no one was sure where they would be planted next. The Branch's numbers had been increased by 150 taken from the ranks of the regular CID and they were arresting many of the conspirators who were receiving hefty prison sentences, which helped. As did the fact that some of the IRA attempts were still failing due to lack of expertise.[2]

Branch member Leonard Burt (who later dealt with our atomic spies) recalled being with Sir Hugh Watts, The Home Office Chief Inspector of Explosives, as he expertly tackled an IRA bomb which had been planted next to an electricity pylon and enquiring nervously whether these things often went wrong as they were being dismantled?

'Sometimes,' said Sir Hugh, as he worked on the improperly wired bomb attached to an electricity pylon, 'But *these* won't.'[3]

By 26 June things were getting personal. It was 10pm on a hot summer night as Robert Fabian, a new Detective Inspector at Vine Street Police Station, was typing out a report on a wobbly typewriter when he heard a massive explosion coming from the direction of Piccadilly Circus. Grabbing his recently-issued gas mask[4] from its hook he ran in that direction, pushed his way through the crowds, scrunching over the broken glass and contents of the broken shop windows then stopped and looked, as they had always been instructed to do.

Amongst the rubble he suddenly spied an intact brown paper parcel. Picking it up he looked around for a bucket of water. No luck. So he took out his pocket knife, cut the string and adhesive tape and unwrapped the parcel. Inside were seven plump sticks of gelignite. He found the fuse, removed it, marched to Vine Street and threw the contents into the fire buckets. This may have not been the sensible correct procedure but it was certainly brave.

There were six explosions in London that night, injuring twenty people. The next day Fabian was part of the raiding team at suspects houses. A couple of days later he received a mysterious phone call inviting him to a Billiard Saloon where he was startled to find the pick of London's Underworld gathered to award him a beautiful bronze medal inscribed:

'To D I Bob Fabian. For Bravery 24.6.39. From the Boys'

He kept the medal in the same drawer as the Kings Medal for Gallantry awarded to him by His Majesty for the same incident.[5]

In July, 1939, the IRA threat to the population was increased with seven bombs in Midlands railway stations and two in London. At Kings Cross station left luggage department one man was severely injured and later died in hospital and two counter attendants were seriously wounded. Five passengers were severely wounded at Victoria Station and a great deal of damage was done to its infrastructure. In Liverpool all barge traffic on the Leeds and Liverpool Canal was halted and the City's main post office wrecked.

On 3 August the IRA announced it would continue its campaign for another two and a half years and deportations of the Irish from Britain increased.

Then came Coventry.

The leader of the Coventry IRA cell was James McCormick who was storing a bomb in his lodgings when IRA Transport Officer, Peter Barnes, brought him the necessary activator, Potassium Chloride, from London.

On 25 August, 1939, the bomb was carried to the target in the basket of a bicycle by IRA volunteer, Joby O'Sullivan. (There was later some diversion of opinion as to whether the intended target had been a police station or an electricity generating plant) but, as Joby is later reported as telling a journalist, the bicycle wheels kept getting jammed in the tram tracks. Which was why he abandoned the bicycle and its lethal load in

Coventry city centre outside a row of shops in busy Broadgate.

The explosion killed five people: John Arnott, aged 15; Elsie Ansell, aged 21; Rex Gentle, aged 30; Gwilym Rowlands, aged 50 and James Clay, aged 82. A further sixty were badly injured.

Elsie Ansell, who had been closest to the blast, was only identifiable by her engagement ring. The total of those killed by the IRA bombs was now ten.

Nine days later the Second World was declared and, in 1940, German aircraft blitzed Coventry several times the most devastating raid being on 14 – 15 November 1940. Inhabitants were later to refer to the IRA bombing as their ' forgotten attack'.

James McCormick and Peter Barnes were tracked down and, with three others, charged with murder of Elsie Ansell. Joby O'Sullivan had caught a train to London and kept a low profile. McCormick and Barnes were found guilty and sentenced to death. There was a concerted attempt to save Barnes and McCormick, 'these innocent men', by Irish leader Eamon de Valera and the U.S., but they were hanged. Regarded as martyrs in Ireland their bodies were repatriated in 1956.[6]

NOTES TO CHAPTER TWENTY-TWO

1. *The Branch* p95-7.
2. *Ibid*, p98-106.
3. *Commander Burt of Scotland Yard,* p113.
4. *Police were early equipped with gas masks in preparation for war.*
5. *Fabian of the Yard*, p76-82.
6. *The Branch,* p107; *Wikipedia*: 1939 Coventry Bombing; The S Plan.

23

The Narrative Reclaimed

Martin Edwards concluded that the detective fiction of the Golden Age was as flawed as the human beings who wrote it but the 'range, quality and inventiveness' of their books did more than give readers enduring pleasure but 'pointed the way forward for writers in the decades that followed'. Like them, today's leading writers regularly reworked elements from real life crimes. What's more, the Detection Club had survived and the writer who had most thrived during those twenty years was the one who began our story – Agatha Christie[1].

Writing in the early 1970s Julian Symons admitted that there was a declining market for the Detective Story but that it had morphed into the Crime Novel. The plot of the Detective Story was based on deception whereas the Crime novel was based on the Psychology of the characters. There were no deceptions and often no detective but if there *was* one he was rarely shown as a brilliant reasoning machine.

Some other differences were that the Detective Story was conservative and the puzzle value *was o*ften high whilst the Crime novel had a varied social attitudes and often questioned some aspects of law, justice, or the way society was run[2].

He also noticed that fewer writers were placing a single character at the centre and there was an increase in those who attempted a realistic view of police work but the problem with these was that if you weren't careful they could end up as dull.[3]

The problem was that the source difficulties remained. British authors successfully tackling the police procedural tended to be either ex police or had worked in police connected jobs – as crime reporters, or Force Press Officers.

A fellow member of the Crime Writers Association who liked to get things right once asked my advice on how to gain more insight on police procedure and I suggested he subscribe to *The Police Review* which carried all the police news and had articles on police-related topics.

He returned even more confused having noticed that every force seemed to do things differently and that there were so many of them. In fact, there were a lot fewer than there had been before the great post war amalgamations but there were still 43 and that was just in England and Wales.

I hadn't been a detective but to assist C.W.A. members I offered to write a page on police matters in the Crime Writers newsletter *Red Herrings*. The editor, Leo Harris, titled it *Locklines*, and I made sure it contained both serious and amusing news culled from sources such as *Police* (the police union mag), *Police Review*, force newspapers, the *New Law Journal*, *Women Police*, and various other UK and US police and law magazines which came my way as a regular contributor to *Police Review*.

I also grilled my police friends and relatives (husband ex-Met served at West End Central, brother a Detective Chief Superintendent in the Cumbria Constabulary where bodies sometimes had to be retrieved from mountain tops or from the bottom of lakes and there was a nuclear power station to protect from possible terrorists.) Not difficult to point up the differences between Cumbria's necessary police procedures with those covering the vice dens of Soho and film premiers of the West End.

My *Red Herrings* page continued for 12 years and was very popular. Not due to my peerless prose but because it filled a need. I only called a halt when I felt I had been out of the police for too long to be a reliable source and because, by then, there was also a *serving* Police Inspector contributing. *Locklines* did keep coming back on and off and a *Lifted Locklines* even made a brief appearance in *The Third Degree,* the Mystery Writers of America's newsletter.

Detective Inspector Jack Henry joined the Metropolitan Police in time to help rescue the victims of one of the first Zeppelin Raids on London during the Great War and retired in 1939, taking over as landlord of a pub in Hampstead. But he was not leaving The Yard behind him. His time as a Divisional Detective Inspector in the West End had allowed him much contact with the Theatrical and Sporting World. Firstly via his work. Such as when all the musical instruments were stolen from Harry Roy's Band or the time pearls and a fur coat went missing from the Adelphi Theatre dressing room of famous actress Gladys Cooper. Contact, too, when Henry was making arrangements for the CID Smoking Concerts.

All this could be glimpsed in his book, *Detective Inspector Henry's Famous Cases,* Chapter 22: *My Adventures with the Stars.* Oddly, you would search the book in vain for the likenesses of these stars, every illustration being a photograph of our author – either whilst involved with said cases or just the man himself as a youthful constable or a boxer in snug shorts. There is even (in more mature mode): 'A Characteristic Study: Jack Henry in Reflective Mood'.

Clearly, Henry was a man good at selling himself but also, it seems, in making contacts. Consequently, even before he retired he had become a character, *Barton of the Yard,* in a series of semi-authentic BBC playlets under the title *What Price Crime?* which featured Henry 'as a real detective in contrast to the sleuth of fiction'. After going out nationally and regionally they were then recorded and broadcast three times 'to the Empire' causing Henry's postbag to oblige him to 'call in a secretary'.

A film was even in the offing but Adolf put paid to that. But Barton went on to more series and Henry began appearing in various other BBC programmes such as *In Town Tonight; Sunday Parlour Games* and *Strange to Relate.* In 1945, came another book, *What Price Crime?* – a mix of mulling over the causes of crime alongside stories of typical cases but this time not *all* of the action photographs featured Jack Henry.

As for Detective Inspector Robert Fabian. He had joined the Metropolitan Police in 1921 so, in 1939, still had some time to serve. Therefore, it was to be 1953 before Ex-Detective *Superintendent* Robert Fabian's book, *Fabian of the Yard,* was published. Police autobiographies were tending to be less inclined to begin each story with them being called to a crime then to take you step by step into the investigation in police procedural fashion. This change was particularly evident in Ex-Detective Superintendent Robert Fabian's book. The stories were well written, and included interesting detail and began by thrusting you into the narrative at an earlier stage, often from the point of view of the victim.

In my particular (1955) copy the illustrations depict the incidents as in the popular new television series, *Fabian of the Yard,* with actor Bruce Seton playing the Fabian role. The series ran to 36 half-hour episodes and at the end of each the actor would morph into the real Fabian, who would explain what had happened to the real-life participants. It is considered to be the earliest police procedural to be shown on British TV and went on to be shown in the U.S. under the title of *Fabian of Scotland Yard* or *Patrol Car*[4]. The narrative had been reclaimed.

NOTES FOR CHAPTER TWENTY-THREE

1. *The Golden Age of Murder*, p431
2. *Bloody Murder*, p173-176
3. *Ibid*, p197-201
4. Wikipedia: Fabian of the Yard

Bibliography

Allason, Rupert, THE BRANCH, A History of the Metropolitan Special Branch 1883-1983 (Secker & Warburg, 1983)

Arrow, Charles, *ROGUES AND OTHERS*, (Duckworth, 1926)

Ascoli, David, *THE QUEEN'S PEACE: The Origins and Development of the Metropolitan Police* (Hamish Hamilton, 1979)

Begg, Paul, & Skinner, Keith, THE SCOTLAND YARD FILES 150 Years of the CID 1842-1992 (Headline, 1992)

Browne, Douglas G and Tullett E V, *BERNARD SPILSBURY His Life and Cases* (The Companion Book Club, 1952)

Brust, Harold, *IN PLAIN CLOTHES Further Memoirs of a Political Police Officer* (Stanley Paul & Co,1937)

Bunker, John, *FROM RATTLE TO RADIO*, (K A F Brewin Books, 1988)

Burt, Leonard, *COMMANDER BURT OF SCOTLAND YARD*, (Pan Books, 1962)

Carlin, Francis, *REMINISCENCES OF AN EX-DETECTIVE*, (Hutchinson)

Cherrill, Fred, *CHERRILL OF THE YARD* (Odhams Press Ltd,

The Popular Book Club)

Christie, Agatha, *AGATHA CHRISTIE AN AUTOBIOGRAPHY* (Harper Collins, 1993) Christie, Agatha, *MURDER ON THE LINKS, (Harper, 2001)*

Coroner's Society, *Notes for the Guidance of Coroners Officers* (E G Berryman, 1921)

Critchley, T A, *A HISTORY OF POLICE IN ENGLAND AND WALES, (Constable, 1979)*

Curran, John, *AGATHA CHRISTIE'S MURDER IN THE MAKING,* (Harper Collins, 2011)

Dilnot, George, *NEW SCOTLAND YARD, (Thomas Nelson, 1938)*

Dilnot, George, *TRIUMPHS OF DETECTION?* (Geoffrey Bles,1929)

Edwards, Martin, *CAPITAL CRIMES*: Editor, (British Library Classics, 2015) Edwards, Martin, *THE GOLDEN AGE OF MURDER,* (Harper Collins, 2015)

Fabian, Robert, *FABIAN OF THE YARD, (Heirloom Modern World Library, 1955)*

Ferrier, J K, *CROOKS AND CRIME* (Seeley, Service & Co, 1928)

Fido, Martin, *THE MURDER GUIDE TO LONDON, (Grafton, 1986)*

Fido, Martin, & Skinner, Keith, *THE OFFICIAL ENCYCLOPEDIA OF SCOTLAND YARD,* (Virgin Books,1999)

Fitch, Herbert T, *MEMOIRS OF A ROYAL DETECTIVE,* (Hurst & Blackett Ltd., 1936)

Gaute J H H & Odell Robin, *THE MURDERERS' WHO'S WHO* (Pan Books, 1980)

Gaute, J H H & Odell, Robin, THE MURDER WHATDUNIT? (Harrap, 1982)

Giles F T, *OPEN COURT* (Cassell, 1964)

Goddard, Henry, MEMOIRS OF A BOW STREET RUNNER, (Museum Press, 1956)

Hambrook, Walter, *HAMBROOK OF THE YARD*, (Robert Hale, 1937)

Henry, Jack, *DETECTIVE INSPECTOR HENRY'S FAMOUS CASES, (Hutchinson & Co)*

Henry, Jack, *WHAT PRICE CRIME?, (Hutchinson,1945)*

Honeycomb, Gordon, *THE MURDERS OF THE BLACK MUSEUM 1870-1970*, (Bloomsbury Books,1992)

Horwell, John E, *HORWELL OF THE YARD,* (Andrew Melrose, 1947)

Howe, Sir Ronald, THE STORY OF SCOTLAND YARD, (New English Library, 1965)

Keating H R F, *WHODUNIT?*: Editor, (W H Smith, 1982)

Kirby, Dick, *The Peeler*, (Friends of the Met Museum Historical Collection, Issue 7, 2002)

Lane, Brian, THE ENCYCLOPEDIA OF FORENSIC SCIENCE, (Magpie Books, 2004)

Leach, Charles E, ON TOP OF THE UNDERWORLD, (Sampson Low, 1933)

Lock, Joan, *DREADFUL DEEDS AND AWFUL MURDERS*, (Barn Owl Books, 1990); *THE BRITISH POLICEWOMAN:*

HER STORY, (Robert Hale, 1979); *SCOTLAND YARD CASEBOOK,* (Robert Hale, 1993); *LADY POLICEMAN,* (Michael Joseph, 1968); *TRULY CRIMINAL: A Crime of Consequence,* (The History Press, 2015)

Martienson, Anthony, *CRIME AND THE POLICE,* (Penguin, 1953)

Morrish, Reginald, *POLICE AND CRIME DETECTION TODAY,* (Oxford University Press, 1940)

Moss, Alan & Skinner, Keith, *SCOTLAND YARD FILES: Milestones in Crime Detection,* (The NationalArchives 2006)

Moylan, J F, *SCOTLAND YARD AND THE METROPOLITAN POLICE,* (Putnam, 1929)

Paul, Philip, *MURDER UNDER THE MICROSCOPE,* (Macdonald, 1990)

Rahn, B J, *THE REAL WORLD OF SHERLOCK,* (Amberly Publishing, 2015)

Rawlings, William, *A CASE FOR THE YARD,* (John Long, 1961)

Rose, Andrew, *THE WOMAN BEFORE WALLACE* (Picador,2013)

Scott, Sir Harold, with Philippa Pearce, *FROM INSIDE SCOTLAND YARD,* (Andre Deutsch, 1963)

Sillitoe, Sir Percy, *CLOAK WITHOUT DAGGER,* (Cassell & Co. 1955)

Smith, P J, *CON MAN (*Herbert Jenkins, 1938)

Symons, Julian, *BLOODY MURDER from the Detective Story*

to the Crime Novel: a History, (Faber and Faber, 1972)

Thorogood, Julia, MARJORIE ALLINGHAM, A BIOGRAPHY, (William Heinemann, 1991)

Thorpe, Arthur, CALLING SCOTLAND YARD, (Allan Wingate, 1954)

Tullett, Tom, FAMOUS CASES OF SCOTLAND YARD'S MURDER SQUAD, (Triad/Granada, 1981)

Wensley, Frederick Porter, DETECTIVE DAYS, (Cassell, 1931)

Whittington-Egan, Richard, THE ORDEAL OF RICHARD YALE DREW, (George G Harrap & Co, 1972)

Willis, Chris, THE FEMALE SHERLOCK' Lady Detectives in Victorian and Edwardian Fiction, (Birkbeck College Dissertation, January, 2000)

Wilson, Colin & Pitman, Patricia, ENCYLOPEDIA OF MURDER, (Pan Books, 1984)

Wyles, Lilian, A WOMAN AT SCOTLAND YARD, (Faber & Faber, 1951)

Acknowledgements

Much gratitude to Martin Edwards for his excellent *The Golden Age of Murder*, which triggered the idea of this contrasting tome and which I have leaned on heavily for the fictional sections that introduce the latest new writers.

Two other leading authorities on the detective story came to my aid. They are the late Julian Symons and the late H R F Keating. Adding a different flavour are the launchings their publishers gave the new writers and the critics' reactions to their books.

As for the reality sections, for that there was my own previous works in the field and that of other non-fiction crime writers, plus front-line news from the real-life police detectives of the time for they, too, wrote books – for which I am most grateful.

INDEX

Printed in Great Britain
by Amazon

87385431R00169